THE ILLUSTRATED HISTORY OF
SOUTHAMPTON'S SUBURBS

JIM BROWN

DB PUBLISHING

First published in Great Britain in 2004 by
The Breedon Books Publishing Company Limited
Breedon House, 3 The Parker Centre,
Derby, DE21 4SZ.

Reprinted 2007

This paperback edition published in Great Britain in 2013 by
DB Publishing, an imprint of JMD Media Ltd

ISBN 978-1-78091-326-1

Printed and bound in the UK by Copytech (UK) Ltd
Peterborough.

THE ILLUSTRATED HISTORY OF
SOUTHAMPTON'S SUBURBS

Contents

Acknowledgements

No author writes in isolation as the difficult process of writing a book needs the active support of a wide circle of people. In this instance I am deeply indebted to the following: Ian Abrahams and the Committee of Bitterne Local History Society for unrestricted access to their vast photographic library; Alastair Arnott, Curator of Local Collections, who initiated my involvement in this project; Joan Holt, for invaluable assistance with proof reading and advice; Janet Keep, Ordnance Survey, for allowing me to reproduce their maps, under reference NC/03/17894; my Editor, Susan Last, for her support and encouragement; Alan G.K. Leonard, who patiently checked my rough drafts and offered constructive advice; Keith Marsh, for his help on Harefield; Keith Le May, for generously allowing me to seriously plagiarise his unpublished personal researches into Thornhill; Derek Smith and Barry Fry, for their assistance regarding Southampton Container Terminal; Maureen Webber, for access to the Henry Brain Collection; Sue Woolgar, and staff of the Southampton City Archives, especially Jo Smith and Susan Hill, for their unfailing readiness to help.

And to the following, who kindly allowed me to reproduce their photos or illustrations:

Southampton Archive Services; *Southern Daily Echo*; The Hampshire & Isle of Wight Trust for Maritime Archaeology; Jonathan Bunn; Vince Davies; Bill Haythorne (Edmund Nuttal Ltd); Peter Heard; Andrew Kent (Port Director, Associated British Ports); Joan Holt; Keith Le May; Bill Monk; Bill Moore; Dolly O'Beirne; Steve Parker (R.J. Parker & Son Ltd); Joy Plummer; Dorothy Prior; Margaret Wallace and Bill White.

The unattributed illustrations are either photographs taken by me or are from my personal collection, some of which were made by companies or individuals that no longer exist or who I have been unable to trace. If I have thus in any way inadvertently infringed somebody's copyright I apologise and hope they will excuse me in the cause of promoting interest in and the sharing of our local heritage.

Last, and by no means least, I am grateful to my wife Marion, not only for her initial proof-reading but for her tolerance of my sustained absences immersed in the depths of my word processor or out researching, without which the book would not have been possible.

J.W.M. Brown

Introduction

ONE definition of a suburb is 'a usually residential area or community on the edge of a city or town'. This initially created a problem when attempting to define those of the modern City of Southampton, as one first had to define the city itself. With the inclusion of its suburbs it is an area in the extreme south of the country, just north of the sheltering Isle of Wight, and measures approximately six by four miles, with a population of over 217,000.

There have been three distinct locations that can be considered as forerunners of the modern Southampton: the confined first-century Roman port in the north-east, the sprawling Saxon township in the south-east and the mediaeval walled town in the south-west. Of these only the last survives as the true heart of the old town and for the purposes of this book this, with its immediate surrounds, is treated as the main inner city area. The earlier locations, together with the subsequent expansions into surrounding areas, are therefore all treated as suburbs.

There have also been many district boundary alterations over the years, due to political, ecclesiastical and postal area changes, and the modern boundaries have become somewhat blurred. Arbitrary decisions have therefore had to be made as to what and where information should be included. The reader may well ask, 'What about my area?' and if it is not specifically mentioned or covered one

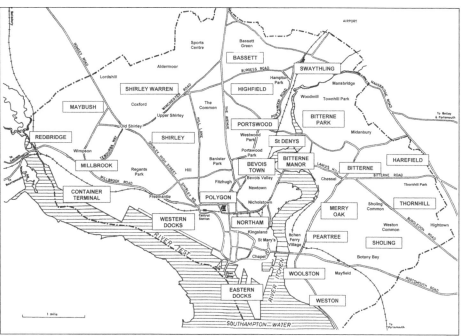

Plan of Southampton's Suburbs and Districts.

can only apologise. However, the ensuing brief history of Southampton may satisfy the curiosity of most readers.

It must be added that limitations of space mean that this book does not aim to provide a definitive history of the City or individual suburbs. Of necessity it is merely a brief description of its growth, with a concluding guide to further in-depth reading at the end of each chapter for those wishing to know more about that particular suburb. Publications covering Southampton as a whole are listed at the end of the 'Brief History of Southampton' chapter. There are also too many topics of historical interest for them to be all included. If I have failed to mention your special interest I can only trust you will find it in the publications I have mentioned. I have tried to include aspects that are not commonly known or are of particular interest.

Southampton has been blessed with numerous excellent 19th and 20th-century local historians, with many continuing to research and publish their results. I have endeavoured to digest the fruit of their labours and reproduce it in a hopefully palatable form, in the hope that you enjoy reading it and are encouraged to delve further into the enthralling history of my home town.

A Brief History of Southampton

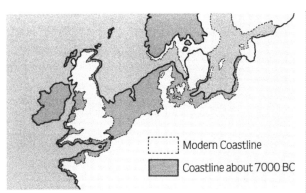

9,000 years ago today's United Kingdom was truly an integral part of mainland Europe as the English Channel and North Sea had not yet formed. It was possible for hunters to travel overland from the heart of Europe and the Scandinavian countries and settle here. When the rising sea levels flooded the deep Solent valley the hilly area in the central extreme south became the Isle of Wight. *(Hampshire and Wight Trust for Maritime Archaeology)*

THE source of Southampton's importance as a premier port, once aptly signposted 'The Gateway to The World', can be traced back to the start of the global warming 10,000 years ago that ended the last Ice Age. Prior to that Britain was truly part of Europe; it was an integral part of that land mass with the entire south-east coast joined to northern France, Germany and Denmark. The English Channel and North Sea had not yet formed and small streams to the east and west and a deep valley to the south enclosed the area of the future Southampton. On the south side of this valley was a diamond-shaped large hill, beyond which was a small stretch of sea leading to the north coast of what we now know as Portugal.

The thick ice sheets melted and, relieved from this great weight, land in northern Britain actually rose, forcing down the lowlands between the south coast and the Netherlands. At the same time the melting ice raised sea levels, flooding the vast lowland areas. The eventual result, by about

This artist's mediaeval view, probably Phillip Brannon's, may well be a romantic one. Following the town walls around anti-clockwise from the square-looking Bargate in the centre left, one can pick out Arundel Tower in the extreme left corner, West Gate to the right of centre and God's House Tower in the upper right. Southampton Castle, with its outer bailey, is very prominent, with the spires of Holy Rood and St Michael's to its right.

The Bargate c.1936. Southampton's symbol, the ancient Bargate, was the northern entrance of the old town. The original Norman construction was a plain semi-circular headed archway, about 10 feet wide, with a watchman's room overhead. It was added to in the 14th century and subject to several restorations over the subsequent centuries. It is here that the Corporation received a toll for goods passing over the Bargate's drawbridge. Above the central arch is the former town hall, 52 feet long and 21 feet wide, once used as a court of justice. This view shows the rear of All Saints Church, with its high cupola, built in 1792 and destroyed in World War Two. Pembroke Square has been demolished on the left to give a southern approach around the Bargate and a police officer is needed to see the northbound traffic and electric trams through the central arch. *(Peter Heard)*

as one of Britain's major ports.

The first port, however, was of a comparatively minor nature, located in the area known today as Bitterne Manor, to the east of the City. Local custom maintains this was the first-century Roman trans-shipment port of Clausentum, but some historians dispute this. However, this early port, whatever its name, with its supporting markets and trading networks, disappeared with the end of Roman rule at the beginning of the fifth century.

Little is known of the initial 'Dark Ages' that followed the exodus of the Roman army, but by the end of that century the Anglo-Saxons had left their German homelands and settled along the south coast. Their gradual expansion led to the creation of the kingdom of Wessex in this southern area, under Cerdic. He had sailed up Southampton Water in about 495 AD, landing between nearby Calshot and Lepe.

The ensuing important commercial township of 'Hamwih' (the original fortified centre), or 'Hamwic' (the riverside trading settlement that surrounded it), was well established by the beginning of the eighth century. It was a densely populated town in the south-eastern Northam area of the City, and included the modern districts of St Mary's, Kingsland and Chapel.

Its contemporaries also knew the ninth-century settlement as 'Hám-tún', the element 'Hám' being Old English for 'home' and 'tún' a man-made enclosure, in this case surrounding an important administrative centre. This reflected the town's reputation as a centre of royal administration and its importance is shown by the name 'Hamptun-

6,000 BC, was the transformation of the small east/west streams into the deeper rivers Itchen and Test; the deep valley into the internationally known Solent and the diamond-shaped hill into the Isle of Wight.

The 'hunter-gatherers' gradually took advantage of these changes and primitive settlements developed in the Southampton area, by then covered with woodland and dense undergrowth. Bronze Age and Iron Age burial mounds or barrows to the north of the present town are evidence of this occupation. Invaders from Gaul arrived from across the Channel in around 500 BC, bringing their iron tools into use, and many relics of this period have been found during local excavations.

The dramatic geographical changes, with the influence of the combined 'bottleneck' effect of the Isle of Wight and Straits of Dover, gave rise to the now famous 'double high water', where the high water stands for two hours and with up to 18 hours of rising water in every 24. This set the scene for Southampton's subsequent development

This life-size portrait of Thomas Macklin (1749–1824), one of the first Masters of the 'Antient Lodge No.174', was painted in 1804 by Tobias Young and still hangs in the Masonic Hall, Albion Place. This was Southampton's first Masonic Lodge, formed in 1772, which met at the Vine Inn in the lower High Street. Macklin was a 'Peruke [wig] Maker, Hairdresser, Perfumer and Toyman' with premises at 151 High Street, destroyed in the 1940 Blitz. These premises were directly opposite the Star Inn (which survived the war), from where coaches ran daily to London, Salisbury, Portsmouth, Bath and Bristol.

scire' given to the surrounding county area. (The Norman who compiled the Domesday Book in 1086 called it 'Hantescire', giving rise to the abbreviation 'Hants' for Hampshire to this day). The first mention of 'South' added to Hamtun appears in 962 when King Eadgar granted the royal dues of 'Suth-hamtune' to the monastery of Abingdon. This was almost certainly done to differentiate it from the Midlands Hamtun that was then developing into a shire town, thus accounting for the modern names of Northampton and Southampton.

The general economic depression in northern Europe in the ninth century, coupled with ever increasing Viking raids on the town, led to its decline and by the 10th century the inhabitants had left the low-lying ground to the east and moved to the more protected high ground in the west, near the River Test. However, it is very likely that this new location still attracted the attention of Viking raiders in the 10th and early 11th century. The town possessed some status as a port during this period, as excavations have revealed much evidence of international trade. It also enjoyed royal interest, as shown by the proclamation in the town in 1014 of Cnut as king. Its important borough status is confirmed by the presence of its mint, with the first silver pennies (sceatta) struck with the name of Hamtun produced in the reign of Athelstan (924–939). These two monarchs are recalled in Canute Road, near the Docks, and Athelstan Road, on the opposite bank of the River Itchen.

Dramatic changes came about following the Norman invasion, in the year that every scholar should know. The subsequent Domesday survey of 1086 showed that Southampton's fortunes had continued, albeit with a smaller population of around 773 people, considerably fewer than the Middle Saxon port some 200 years earlier. This population was by then divided into two distinct communities, French and English, reflected in the two main north-south streets called French Street and English Street; the latter is now the High Street. William the Conqueror's army fortified the town perimeter with earthen banks, with a ditch beyond, and a massive stone archway was erected to protect the northern approach to the town. This was enlarged in the 12th century to create today's imposing 'Bargate', guarded by its large lead lion sentinels that date from 1743 and replace earlier wooden ones.

The Conquest brought steadily increasing prosperity to the port, which provided a direct link between Normandy and England. Much wine was imported from France, resulting in the construction of massive wine vaults, many of

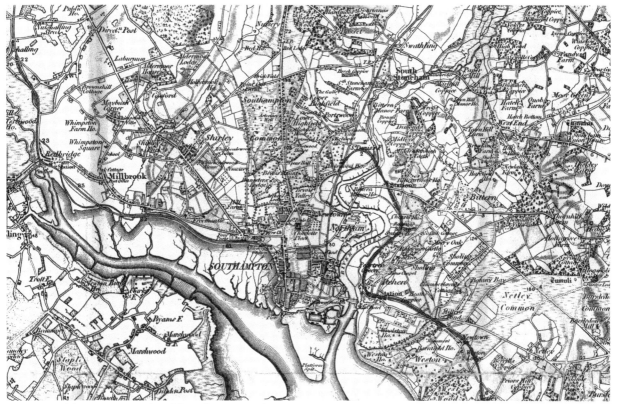

1864 map of the town. *(Reproduced from the 1864 Ordnance Survey map. NC/03/17894)*

Southampton High Street *c.*1895, looking towards the Bargate with the bow windows of the Georgian Dolphin Hotel on the right. Just behind it is the spire of St Lawrence Church, built in 1760 and demolished in 1925 as redundant. In 1801 Sir H.C. Englefield said of the church 'it does not contain a single object either of beauty or antiquity'. Virtually all the buildings on the left, above the bank on the corner, were destroyed in the Blitz of 1940.

Weymouth Terrace in the far centre background, photographed from the southern end of Forest View, *c.*1900. It was demolished during the construction of the Portland Terrace Ring Road in the mid-1960s. *(Henry Brain Collection – Maureen Webber)*

The same view in 2003. The massive new West Quay shopping complex, constructed in 1999, now takes up the former stretch of open water.

which still exist today. By the reign of Henry II, in the middle of the 12th century, an imposing castle with a bailey wall around it had been constructed, in the area of today's Lansdown Hill. This is evidence of a royal interest in the town, which continued to prosper. However, at 9am on the morning of Sunday 4 October 1338, following a declaration of war with France, the town was invaded without warning by a fleet of French, Genoese and Sicilians. The town was sacked and it is believed that some inhabitants were attacked inside St Michael's Church. The town was not then entirely walled and consequently further strengthening took place, over the following decades, at the conclusion of which the Bargate was enlarged, the walls built up to a height of 30ft and completely encircling the town, with seven gateways, 29 towers and double moats to the north and east for extra defence.

Trade expanded, with an increased export of wool from the Hampshire downlands and import of wine from France. This was in spite of the terrible Black Death epidemic that had entered the country through Southampton in 1348. One of the substantial stone wool houses, now the Maritime Museum, can be seen at the bottom of

Bugle Street. Throughout the latter years of the 14th century attention was turned mainly to defence and war preparations.

In 1404 the French raided the nearby Isle of Wight and threatened the town. In 1415, as though in retaliation, Southampton served as the main embarkation port for Henry V, who passed through the West Gate en route to his victorious campaign at Agincourt. As part of its military potential Southampton also served as a shipbuilding centre, with a special dock constructed near the Town Quay. Among the famous ships constructed there was the *Grace Dieu*, the largest clinker-built ship of the Middle Ages.

By the middle of the 15th century the town was at the height of its success and was the third largest port in England. Suburbs were growing to the north and east and the residents enjoyed the benefits of extensive international trade, especially wool, through the port. In 1447 Henry VI made a Charter whereby the town became the 'Town and County of the Town of Southampton', with its own Sheriff as distinct from the Sheriff of Hampshire. This was an important honour and saved the town from various financial burdens. A further honour came in 1451 when the King bestowed on the Mayor the office of Admiral of the Port, with jurisdiction extending from Lymington in the west to Portsmouth in the east. A silver oar, the symbol of this Admiralty, is carried before the Mayor to this day on all ceremonial occasions.

Southampton's 1454 *Terrier* provides a 15th-century record that is probably unique for any town in Europe, let alone England. It is a very detailed survey of the town within the walls, giving a street-by-street description of all properties and their owners or occupiers and provides a precise description of the town's defences. Wealthy merchants, many of whom were Italian, had built substantial houses, and as with most mediaeval townships, there were concentrations of particular trades in various areas. Overall, a picture is painted of a busy, bustling and prosperous community.

By the mid-16th century, however, a decline had set in, due mainly to political upheavals in Italy. The port then changed from a major international centre to a small market town, with trade depending more on the Channel Islands. There was a short-lived boom in trade with France, Spain, Portugal and the Azores during the third quarter of the century, with an increase in shipbuilding, but the war with Spain provided a lucrative opportunity for some of its citizens – privateering!

A more lasting benefit came from the immigration of Walloon refugees from France and the Netherlands. This brought craftsmen in weaving and woolcombing, and their St Julian's Church, known as the French Church, at God's House, Winkle Street, stands as their testament to this day. Southampton then entered the end of the century with only a modest prosperity, based on its cloth industry and a continuing market centre for southern Hampshire.

The Tudor age gave rise to a sustained growth

A rare view of the Grand Theatre in 1905, built on the site of the Marlands in 1898. Standing outside the front entrance are the Sole Lessee & Manager, Frederick Mouillot, and the Resident Manager Sidney Paxton. Patrons queuing in the adjoining Windsor Terrace would be tempted by the sight and smells of Plested's pie shop and few could resist a snack while waiting. Damaged during the World War Two, the Grand reopened in December 1950 but its last performance was in October 1959. It was demolished in March 1960 and replaced by a large office block. *(Peter Heard)*

in the town's population, from about 1,500 in 1454 to 4,200 in 1596. (This was in spite of a severe fatal influenza epidemic and outbreaks of bubonic plague during that period.) The flood of incomers attracted to the town included a considerable number of artisans and craftsmen, but its financial affairs still failed to show any real improvement.

The next event of interest in the town helped to

Lower Southampton in 1923, taken from the top of the Royal Yacht Club at the bottom of Bugle Street. It shows the end of Cuckoo Lane on the left, with the steps leading to the top of the Old Walls and Westgate. On the upper right is the large block of St Michael's Municipal Lodging House, erected in 1898 and demolished in 1972. The houses in the centre foreground are in Westgate Terrace, destroyed during World War Two. *(Peter Heard)*

change the history of the world! On 15 August 1620, as a result of the persecution of Puritans by James I, 120 brave souls departed from Southampton in the *Mayflower* and *Speedwell* to seek their freedom of worship. The Pilgrims had walked through the Westgate to board their ships moored off the West Quay and would have walked the cobbled streets of the walled town while their ships were being prepared. It was only because the *Speedwell* sprang a leak that Plymouth was later able to capitalise on the venture, the true privilege goes to Southampton.

When the Civil War broke out in 1642 the sympathies of Southampton's merchant class were probably with Parliament and a Roundhead garrison moved into the town unopposed. Royalists advanced as far as nearby Redbridge the following year, where they broke down the bridge over the River Test to cut off supplies from the west, but they progressed no further. The town suffered no real ill effects from this unhappy period and the return of Charles II brought the town's loyalists to the fore. The coronation on 23 April 1661 was celebrated with the firing of 'great guns' and it was said that the 'four town water conduits ran with claret wine'! It is not known just how long this unusual expression of loyalty functioned. Such happiness, however, did not last for long.

The unusually hot June of 1665 brought with it the scourge of the Great Plague and it spread through the town with terrifying rapidity. It is said that 1,700 inhabitants died of the pestilence, with consequent disruption to the town's economy. This improved slightly at the end of the century with a revival in shipbuilding, mainly centred on Northam and Chapel, but the town's fortunes were not really transformed until a spring of chalybeate water was discovered on a site just north of the Bargate, overlooking the River Test. The water contained strong elements of iron and sulphur and was considered to have powerful medicinal effects.

This coincided with a visit from Frederick, Prince of Wales, in the summer of 1750. He bathed in the western shore and found the seawater 'salubrious and invigorating'. Where the Prince led the nobility and gentry soon followed, and the local residents were quick to seize the advantage. They lost no time in laying out spacious Spa Gardens, with a Reading Room, Botanical Garden and new Assembly Rooms with a Ball Room. The town rapidly developed into an extremely fashionable spa, the hotels flourished, royalty made frequent visits and 'new elegant assemblages of genteel houses' were erected within the town walls. Great improvements were made in the water supplies; better lighting was installed and new paving laid and the town was at the height of its elegance.

Freemasonry came to the town on 22 April 1772 with the formation of 'Antient Lodge No.174', meeting at the Vine Tavern at the bottom of Southampton High Street. This Lodge was the forerunner of the modern Royal Gloucester Lodge No.130, Southampton's senior Lodge and sponsor of many of the City's present day Masonic Lodges. The outskirts of the town became more attractive to the upper echelons of society at this time and the completion of the first Northam Bridge, in 1799, opened up a direct eastern route from the town, allowing great estates to develop on that side of the river.

However, when the Prince of Wales became Prince Regent in 1811 he found Brighton more attractive and the coaches that had once filled Southampton now travelled to Brighton. The town once again passed into a period of decline.

What then passed for 'hi-tech' equipment, however, saved the day. The first steamboat carried the mails from Southampton to Cowes on the Isle of Wight in 1822 and in 1833 a new and imposing pier to assist this new traffic was opened by the Duchess of Kent, accompanied by her daughter, 14-year-old Princess Victoria. London merchants and shipping companies considered the construction of docks at the port to further develop the new 'steam-propelled ships' now making their appearance. A Southampton Dock Company was soon formed and in 1838 the foundation stone was laid amid much ceremony.

By 1840 the entire railway line from London to the Southampton Terminus Station was finally constructed, completing an essential communication system. The port entered its greatest change of fortune two years later when the Peninsular & Oriental Steam Navigation Company and the Royal Mail Steam Packet Company came to the town, setting the seal on its commercial viability. A large Inner Dock was completed in 1851 and international trade began to escalate. The port also became a prime location for the large-scale embarkation of troops for wars in the Crimea, Egypt, the Sudan and South Africa.

By 1901, when Queen Victoria died, Southampton's population had risen from 19,000 in 1831 to 104,000. Much of this increase was due to the absorption of Bitterne Park, Banister, Freemantle and Shirley into the town in 1895, consolidating the inevitable outward growth of residential accommodation. However, the storm

A view from the top of Marland House c.1988, at the start of the construction of the new Marlands Shopping Centre, opened in September 1991. The cleared foundations in the right foreground are on the site of the former coach station, with Windsor Terrace to the left. Manchester Street's remaining terrace, centre right, is still preserved inside the Shopping Centre, but the twin tower blocks behind them were swept away in 1998 for the construction of the modern West Quay Shopping Centre.

clouds of war gathered again and in 1914 the port once more assumed its strategic rôle as a centre for embarkation, for what the Kaiser called 'Sir John French's contemptible little army'. Over the ensuing war years over seven million troops, 800,000 horses, 177,000 vehicles and 14,000 guns passed through the port – a noteworthy achievement.

After the war the pace of industrial development increased, with shipbuilding and repairing by Thornycrofts, Harland and Wolff, White Brothers and others; cable manufacturer Pirelli, and tobacco manufacturer BAT, all contributing to opportunities and the overall prosperity of the town. The docks had also gradually and consistently expanded during the preceding years, but now a massive increase in dock space was required to cope with the ever-demanding transatlantic passenger and other cruise liners. The never to be forgotten White Star liner *Titanic* had sailed from Southampton on its ill-fated maiden voyage in 1912, a tragedy that struck at the heart of the town. Few streets had remained untouched by a loss as over 550 of the crew lived here with their families.

The town's need for expansion was satisfied in 1920, and its area almost doubled, when it incorporated Woolston, Sholing, Bitterne and Bitterne Manor east of the River Itchen and Swaythling and Bassett to the north of the town. To avoid duplication of street names, many were changed during the various expansions and full details of these are given on page 156. The town's population had grown from 13,353 in 1821, more than quadrupled to 65,000 at the turn of the century and by 1927 stood at 165,000. This need for housing was met in part by a number of estates developed in a distinctive style by an outstanding local architect, Herbert Collins (1885–1975), and his impressive work can still be seen.

The 1930s saw vast areas adjoining the River Test reclaimed, to construct the 'New Docks' in the west of the town. This produced a further 7,000 feet of deep-water quays and a massive 1,200-foot long King George V graving dock. Inland, an impressive Civic Centre was constructed on the site of the Marlands recreation ground and an imposing Sports Centre developed to the north of the town. The borough had entered a further period of prosperity.

This was shattered following the outbreak of World War Two, with the consequent terrible destruction of the heart of the town and docks. Prior to the *blitzkrieg* unleashed by the Nazis Southampton was in the forefront of receiving the survivors of Dunkirk, with scores of local small boats involved in the rescuing armada. The Docks, of course, were a prime target for the bombers, who also destroyed the Supermarine Works on the Itchen shore. This was the home of the Spitfire, created by their chief designer, R.J. Mitchell. 630 citizens were killed in the war years and nearly 2,000 injured. A total of 4,278 domestic properties were totally destroyed by enemy action and Southampton was littered with bombsites and derelict buildings.

Initial temporary rebuilding soon took place, however, and Southampton gradually recovered, as it had done in previous centuries. The tempo of activity accelerated in the 1950s when roads forged through new routes, tower blocks of flats mushroomed and new shopping and community developments appeared. In 1954 the borough boundaries were once again extended, to the west to include Millbrook and Redbridge, and in the east with Harefield and parts of Thornhill. Two Members of Parliament for the roughly equal constituencies of Itchen and Test, east and west of the River Itchen respectively, then served Southampton. This was a period when a well-maintained four-bedroomed house with three reception rooms could be purchased for around £1,500.

February 1964 saw the ultimate accolade for Southampton, the granting of City status, and the following year one of their long-serving Members

A 1940 view of the horrific consequence of the wartime *blitzkrieg* in the heart of Southampton. *(Southern Daily Echo)*

The same area in 2004, the ruins replaced by an imposing pedestrian precinct.

of Parliament, Dr Horace King, (later Lord Maybray King) was elected Speaker of the House of Commons. However, this was followed in 1967 by the loss of the City Police Force when it amalgamated with Hampshire Constabulary.

The local football team, the Saints, won the FA Cup in 1976, and the scale of their welcome on their City tour had echoes of the celebrations at the end of World War Two! This decade also saw the opening of the massive Itchen Bridge, providing a direct road link across the lower stretch of

the river and easing the terrible peak period congestion of the upper stretch of Northam Bridge. Crucial for the docks' continued importance, and of great benefit to the local economy, was its third dramatic stage of development, the reclamation of the upper River Test and construction of the massive Container Terminal.

In 1982 Southampton Docks played a pivotal rôle in the Falklands War and the sight of the 'Great White Whale', the P&O liner *Canberra*, returning battle-weary and rust-stained, surrounded by an armada of small boats, was one that the many thousands who witnessed it will never forget. This much-loved ship had sailed from the port on its maiden voyage in 1961 and had endeared itself to the town.

By the 1990s Southampton had gained a reputation as the prime centre of trade and commerce on the south coast, and this brought to fruition the massive West Quay shopping centre, currently dominating the western skyline. It was during this decade that Southampton Docks became the number one port for the country's multi-million pound cruising industry and the M3 motorway linking the south coast with London was finally completed.

Southampton entered the 21st century on an optimistic note, in spite of the country's overall economic depression, and at the time of writing the city leisure department is developing a five-year plan to transform the town's rôle as a 'city of culture'. Costing over £90 million, there are proposals for an Olympic-sized 7,000-seat ice rink, a venue for concerts and conferences, a major heritage centre, a cultural quarter in Above Bar and a programme of national and regional events, such as the BT Global Challenge and Volvo Ocean race. Like their ancient City fathers before them, the local authority is continually planning for the future. With a population of over 217,000, with black and ethnic minority groups making up nearly eight percent of its inhabitants and, because of its large university, a higher than average population in the age group 20–24 (12.5% compared to 6% nationally), this planning is subject to constant change.

In conclusion, this ancient and proud City of Southampton, with its fine University, does not have a Lord Mayor, unlike its eastern rival Portsmouth. Neither does it have a Cathedral, as does its northern neighbour Winchester. Hopefully these omissions will be rectified by the time this book is updated for the by then further enlarged Southampton, later in this 21st century!

Further Reading

Arnott, Alastair & Wragg, R. *Images of Southampton,* Breedon Books, 1994.

Arnott, Alastair *Maritime Southampton,* Breedon Books, 2002.

Bissell, Andrew *Southampton's Children of the Blitz,* Red Post, 2001.

Boyd-Smith, Jan and Peter *Southampton, Gateway to England,* Red Post, 2002.

—— *Southampton In Focus,* Steamship Publications, 1996.

Brown, Jim *Henry Brain, A Victorian & Edwardian Photographer,* Bitterne Local History Society, 2000.

Coates, Richard *Hampshire Place Names,* Ensign Publications, 1993.

Cook, Robert *Britain in Old Photographs, Southampton,* Sutton Publishing, 1996.

Davies, Rev. J. Silvester *History of Southampton,* Gilbert & Co., 1883.

Englefield, Sir H.C. *A Walk Through Southampton,* Baker, 1841.

Gadd, Eric *Southampton, On Reflection,* Kingfisher Publications, 1989.

Gale, Allison *The Story Beneath the Solent,* Hampshire & Wight Trust for Maritime Archaeology, 1991.

Gallaher, Tony *A Century of Southampton,* Sutton Publishing, 2000.

—— *Southampton's Inns and Taverns,* T. Gallaher, 1995.

Horne, John *100 Years of Southampton Transport,* City of Southampton, 1979.

Jenkins, Roger *History of the Royal Gloucester Lodge,* 1992.

Kemp, Anthony *Southampton At War 1939–45*, Ensign Publications, 1989.

Kimber, Sir Sidney *Thirty-Eight Years of Public Life in Southampton*, Privately Published, 1949.

Knowles, Bernard *Southampton, The English Gateway*, Hutchinson & Co., 1951.

Leonard, Alan G.K. *Southampton, Images of England*, Tempus, 1997.

—— *Southampton, The Second Selection*, Tempus 2002.

—— *Southampton in Old Picture Postcards*, European Library, 1992.

—— *Stories of Southampton Streets*, Paul Cave Publications, 1984.

—— *More Stories of Southampton Streets*, Paul Cave Publications, 1989.

Mann, John Edgar *Southampton People*, Ensign Publications, 1989.

Moody, Bert *Southampton's Railways*, Waterfront Publications, 1992.

—— *150 Years of Southampton Docks*, Kingfisher Railway Productions, 1988.

Monkhouse, F.J. *A Survey of Southampton and its Region*, The British Association, 1964.

Pannell, J.P.M. *Old Southampton Shores*, David & Charles, Newton Abbot, 1967.

Patterson, A. Temple *A History of Southampton 1700–1914*, Southampton University Press, 1971.

—— *Southampton, A Biography*, Macmillan, 1970.

Peckham, Ingrid *Southampton & D-Day*, Oral History, Southampton City Heritage, 1994.

Platt, Colin *Medieval Southampton*, Routledge & Kegan Paul, 1973.

Rance, Adrian *Southampton, An Illustrated History*, Milestone Publications, 1986.

—— *Shipbuilding in Victorian Southampton*, Southampton University Industrial Archaeology Group, 1981.

Sandell, Elsie M. *Southampton Sketches*, 1948.

—— *Southampton Panorama*, 1958.

—— *Southampton Cavalcade*, 1977.

—— *Southampton Through the Ages*, 1980, all G.F. Wilson & Co.

Stovold, Jan *Bygone Southampton*, Phillimore & Co., 1984.

Velecky, Lubor *Protect It Now – A History of Southampton Commons & Parks Protection Society*, 2000.

Vale, Jessica *The Country Houses of Southampton*, Hampshire Field Club, 1983.

White, Bill, Sheila Jemima and Donald Hyslop *Dream Palaces*, Southampton City Council, 1996.

Williams, David L. *Docks and Ports – Southampton*, Ian Allen Ltd, 1984.

Williams, Robert *Herbert Collins 1885–1975*, Paul Cave Publications, 1985.

Relevant Websites:

Bitterne Local History Society – www.bitterne.net

City of Southampton – www.southampton.gov.uk

Hamble Local History Society – www.pendlebury30.fsnet.co.uk

Hampshire County Council – www.hants.gov.uk

Peartree Green – www.peartreegreen.org

Bassett

including Bassett Green and the Sports Centre

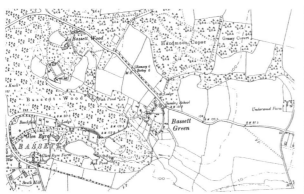

Note the amount of woodland in 1931, with Glen Eyre Farm in the lower left corner. The crematorium has yet to be constructed. *(Reproduced from the 1931 Ordnance Survey map. NC/03/17894)*

BASSETT (originally with only one 't'), part of the parish of North Stoneham, may have got its name from a farming family of that name, known to have once lived in Stoneham. It is, however, equally likely that it derives from an old French word meaning an outcrop of land and that the family name came from their place of residence.

One of the earliest records, the Domesday survey of 1086, places North Stoneham, with 48 recorded inhabitants, in the Mansbridge Hundred. It then belonged to the Abbot of St Peter of Winchester and possessed a church, probably made of wood. This is now the parish church of St Nicholas, instituted in 1248 and well known for its delightful peals of 10 bells. It was once ranked

25th in the country's list of belfries for the number of peals rung in a tower.

Sir Thomas Fleming purchased North Stoneham in 1599 and the family connection has continued to the present day. The last Squire was John Edward Arthur Willis Fleming, who died in 1949, and his ashes are in the family vault in St Nicholas' churchyard.

The original Bassett, at the southern section of North Stoneham, was called Basset Green, but this was eventually shortened to just Basset. An 1899 directory describes the area as 'A pleasant village 2 miles from Southampton and 1½ southwest of North Stoneham and in that parish'. It then had around 150 residents and a small number of commercial premises, mainly nurseries and market gardens.

In 1896 the Basset residents felt they needed their own church and on application to the Fleming Estate the Squire readily granted a gift of

Bassett Green Village is an oasis of tranquillity on the outskirts of the busy port of Southampton and the thatcher's ancient skills are still in evidence.

St Michael and All Angels Church, Bassett Avenue. Its foundation stone was laid in 1897 with the assistance of a legacy and gift of land from the squire, John Fleming. Its east window, depicting Christ, angels and knights, was the first stained-glass design made by the famous artist Frank Salisbury. The fine west window, depicting the Archangel Michael, was donated in 1962 by Hector Young, former Southampton Mayor, in memory of his wife who was killed in the Blitz.

land. The foundation stone of St Michael & All Angels Church was thus laid on 29 September the following year. It was, and remains, a 'chapel of ease' to St Nicholas Parish Church and a Rector was appointed, to live in Basset.

At the end of the century Burgess Street (as it was then called) was the borough's northern boundary and the western Bassett region, either side of Bassett Avenue, was a desirable country area with an ever-increasing scattering of good-quality detached houses. It remains a select residential district to this day. In 1926 a house, described as having a lounge, two reception rooms, four bedrooms, a good domestic office and cellarage, with a pleasant garden and garage, was for sale in Bassett for £2,500.

Bassett (now with the extra 't') was absorbed into the borough in 1920, along with Swaythling and several districts east of the Itchen. This soon opened up the hitherto rural area to developers and among the first was the Swaythling Housing Society, who built about a hundred properties at the lower end of the modern Bassett Green Road, at the eastern side of Bassett. The Society is still responsible for the maintenance of the communal areas and greens. This was the beginning of the Bassett Green Estate, whose principal designer was the renowned architect Herbert Collins. His first Georgian-style houses were built in lower Stoneham Lane, where a plaque dated 1927 is displayed at numbers 25–27.

A new road, Ethelburt Avenue, was constructed to link Stoneham Lane and Bassett Green Road, and it contains three squares of different sizes, all open to the south. The road is not, as one would think, named after an ancient king, but derives from a combination of the Christian names of Herbert and his sister Ethel. Building continued apace, with houses constructed in Leaside Way in 1934, but this ceased when war broke out in 1939, resuming on the east side of Ethelburt Avenue when hostilities ended.

A tender of £83,010 had been accepted in 1931 by Southampton Corporation for the erection of

Burgess Road in 1928, where the last tramway extension from the Junction to Bassett & Portswood is being laid. This view is looking towards Swaythling and shows Miss Longster's bungalow and nursery, since demolished and now the site of Burgess Court Old People's Home. The photo was taken before the erection of Burgess Road Library. *(Norman Gardiner Collection – Bitterne Local History Society)*

Nos 25 and 27 Stoneham Lane in 2004, showing the plaque dated 1927. They are the initial impressive Georgian-style houses built by the architect Herbert Collins at the beginning of the Bassett Green Estate and remain as distinctive as ever.

Ivy-clad Red Lodge, c.1870, at the corner of Winchester Road and Bassett Avenue. This is thought to show the well-known Rogers family who first lived there in around 1829. They ran the nearby Red Lodge Nurseries and their business premises, W.H. Rogers & Son Ltd, Florists, were at 132 High Street in the town. (*Norman Gardiner Collection – Bitterne Local History Society*)

217 council houses on the south-eastern part of the site, with £10,416 agreed for the construction of roads and sewer works. The roads were named after flowers – Lupin, Lobelia and Poppy – and Carnation Road was re-numbered to allow for the new houses built on its extension. This well known 'Flower Estate' was soon extended to include Bluebell, Lilac, Violet, Honeysuckle and other flower roads.

In 1951 the 14-acre Hardmoor Copse in Bassett Green Road was approved as a suitable site for a crematorium. Negotiations for its purchase and work on the design of the building's twin chapels began in 1967 and were completed in 1971. Opened in October 1973, it is set in beautiful undulating natural woodland, augmented by thousands of bulbs and numerous species of woodland flowers.

Southampton's 'capital of sport' is undoubtedly the 300-acre Sports Centre in Bassett, the creation of Alderman Sir Sidney Kimber and opened by the Duke of Kent on 28 May 1938. It has many facilities that are hard to rival and attracts sportsmen and women from near and far. It has artificial ski slopes, an all-weather synthetic running track and two all-weather synthetic grass pitches that provide the largest and finest syn-

The modern Red Lodge, now called Little Oak Hall and for many years the home of the late antiquarian bookseller, Bruce Gilbert, DFC. In 1941 the adjacent nurseries were used by Southampton Police and the Civil Defence as an emergency base. It became their wartime training headquarters and housed the main radio transmitter. (*Norman Gardiner Collection – Bitterne Local History Society*)

The Bassett Hotel, Burgess Road c.1900. This was well known for its gardens with many amusements for children, including 'Miska', a bear brought from Russia as a baby. It escaped in 1877 onto the Common but had to be shot when it became dangerous in 1907. It was then stuffed and put on display. A replacement bear, 'Buster', was shot in 1932 and also placed in a glass case. The hotel was also the original home of the famous celebrity jazz groups that met at the Concorde Club, before it moved to Stoneham Lane. *(Henry Brain Collection – Maureen Webber)*

thetic sports area in the country. The longest run of the second ski slope is 110 metres, with an independent tow giving skiers an easy route back to the top. It also has a nursery slope for beginners and is floodlit at night. There are five soccer pitches; five cricket pitches; 12 tennis courts; two bowling greens; a cycle track; a children's pleasure park; a paddling pool and a boating lake. In pride of place are two golf courses. One is a fine 69 par 18-hole course, measuring 5,683 metres, and the other a 33 par nine-hole course measuring 2,185 metres. It is altogether a most fitting tribute to Sir Sidney Kimber's memory and an excellent amenity for the City's residents.

The modern Bassett therefore has three distinct areas: the more select detached houses to the north, the large council estate to the east and the massive Sports Centre to its west. It also hosts the University's large bio-medical science block, on the site of the former Boldrewood country house at the corner of Burgess Road and Bassett Avenue.

The Bassett Ward currently has a population of around 13,500 and in its high-status area the proportion of managerial and professional workers is roughly twice that of other parts of the city. It remains a desirable area, on the outskirts of the city, but is now dominated by the presence of the nearby ever-expanding Southampton University.

Further Reading

Bakes, Anne *The Parish of North Stoneham & Bassett*, A. Bakes, 1996.
Mann, John Edgar *The Book of the Stonehams*, Halsgrove, 2002.
Williams, Robert *Herbert Collins 1885–1975*, Paul Cave Publications, 1985.

Bevois Town

including Bevois Valley, Newtown and Nicholstown

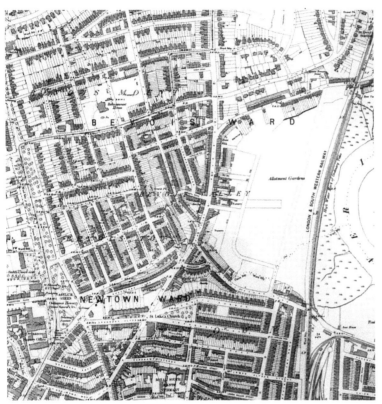

1897 map of Bevois Town and Newtown. *(Reproduced from the 1897 Ordnance Survey map. NC/03/17894)*

THIS district, to the south of Portswood, rises from the western shore of the River Itchen to a stretch of high ground that drops to form a deep valley between Portswood and Newtown. The high ground is believed to have been part of a Roman fort with a steep escarpment and a wide ditch at the bottom. It was one of two Roman stations on the western bank opposite Clausentum, the other having been at Northam. In the early 19th century there used to be a mound to the south-east called Blackberry Mount, part of an old Roman earthwork. This gave its name to the modern Blackberry Terrace that connects Bevois Valley with Newtown via Mount Pleasant Road.

In about 1723 Charles Mordaunt, the 3rd Earl of Peterborough, bought Padwell Farm, which he enlarged and developed into a mansion with extensive gardens. He called it 'Bevis Mount', commemorating the legendary mediaeval hero Sir Bevis. The lower part of his estate, towards the river, became known as Bevis Valley, and this spelling soon became corrupted to Bevois, a spelling that prevailed.

The metrical romance of Sir Bevis of Hampton is thought to have been written by a Southampton Anglo-Norman scribe and it was a 'bestseller' for some centuries. It was translated into Italian and French and first printed in Venice in 1489.

The story itself has several versions, the most common being that Sir Bevis was the son of Guy, Earl of Southampton, and that his step-mother sold him to a merchant who took him to Armenia, where he was sold as a slave. He eventually escaped, fought the King of Armenia's foes and killed a savage boar that had ravaged the land. As a reward, in true romantic fashion, he married the King's daughter, Josian. He was given a magic sword and horse, Mortglay and Arundel, and they set off for England. En route a savage giant, Ascupart, attacked him but he was overcome and became his faithful squire.

One day, after many adventures, Josian was left in a cave while the two men looked for food. Two huge lions came by but didn't attack her as

'The Shear', at the junction of Lodge Road and Thomas Lewis Way, is by sculptor Ellis O'Connell. It soars 30 feet into the skyline and is said to have cost £80,000. It contains nearly seven miles of cable and commemorates the former rope-working industry in the area. It is also meant to symbolise the sword of the legendary Sir Bevois, and the giant Ascupart is thought to be buried in the vicinity.

each other's arms, while the wonder-horse Arundel died in his stable.

Ascupart Street and Bevois Valley commemorate this story and for many years two large panels, depicting the two men, flanked the centre arch of the town's Bargate. They can now be viewed inside the Bargate museum. It is also thought that the two lions guarding the Bargate entrance are connected with the romance of Sir Bevois. The earliest mention of them is in a Court Leet record of 1619, when it was suggested that the carved lions be varnished to prevent them from rotting. The present lead ones were made in 1743.

The legend of Sir Bevois arose again when excavations were made for the Earl of Peterborough's summerhouse in about 1730. Part of a huge human skeleton was uncovered, and this was later thought to be the remains of Sir Bevois. An 18th-century print shows an unidentified tomb standing on Bevois Mount, but this was destroyed and incorporated into the foundations of a cottage, now a shop, at 155 Bevois Valley Road on the corner of Forster Road.

Bevois Mount mansion quickly became a focal point for high society, with the Earl entertaining

they appreciated her beauty and virtue. They therefore took up positions either side of the cave entrance and guarded her until the men returned.

There were many more adventures, with several variations for the ending, the most popular telling how Ascupart died first, followed by Bevis and Josian dying in

Stag Gates at the junction of Lodge Road with The Avenue, 1919. Erected in 1845 by William Betts at the entrance of the driveway to Bevois Mount and presented to Southampton Corporation in 1919 by William Burrough Hill, they were demolished because the width between the pillars made it difficult for two vehicles to pass simultaneously. The removal also made it possible for the double tramline to take a wider curve at this junction and greatly improved the transport situation. The stags were said to have been saved but their whereabouts is an unsolved mystery. *(Norman Gardiner Collection – Bitterne Local History Society)*

The scene is vastly different in 2004 – even the tramlines have vanished!

Bevois Valley Road, *c.*1910. The Wesleyan Methodist Chapel on the left was registered in 1861 and sold in 1962 to become a Sikh temple. *(Norman Gardiner Collection – Bitterne Local History Society)*

such prominent national figures as Jonathan Swift, Voltaire and Alexander Pope, who described the estate as 'beautiful beyond imagination'. The Earl had fashioned winding paths beneath spreading cedars, leading to cool lakes, summerhouses and grottoes. However, he would only allow visitors to enter his garden at high tide because the mud of the River Itchen not only spoilt the view but also gave off an offensive smell!

The Earl died in 1735, followed by his widow in 1755, and Bevois Mount passed to a nephew, John Mordaunt. He erected a marble tablet at the house in memory of his uncle and this is now in Tudor House Museum.

In 1844, after several owners, a contractor who had built the Royal Pier, William Betts, bought the estate. He made extensive alterations and additions to the property and erected the well-known pair of gate pillars surmounted by carved stone stags at The Avenue entrance of the estate's driveway, now Lodge Road. This junction continues to be known as Stag Gates, although the gates have long since vanished.

In 1854 Betts sold the house and a few acres of the garden to J.H. Wolff, a shipping agent, and the rest of the estate to Sampson Payne, an enterprising property speculator. Shortly afterwards the area was developed for housing by the Conservative Land Society and the only reminders of the former estate lie in the names of Peterborough Road, Padwell Road and Mordaunt Road. The house itself, having been in turn

Old Farm House and Mount Pleasant School, 2003. The Old Farm House, 39 Mount Pleasant Road, is a Grade II listed building and dates back to 1611, when it was a working farm-house. This date can be clearly seen in the front wall. One of the earliest written records of the area is a mortgage deed of 1704, when John Winter, a shipwright, borrowed £617 on the security of Northam Farm. The farm changed in 1843 when it became a Panton's Wareham Brewery beer house. Mount Pleasant School opened in 1898 with 1,233 pupils and is still active today, serving a local population of mixed ethnic origins.

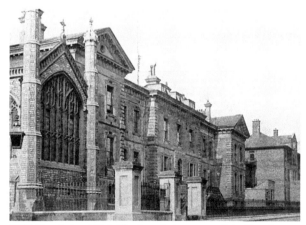

RSH Hospital, *c.*1925. The foundation stone of the Royal South Hants Infirmary, fronting the site of the former Antelope Cricket Ground, was laid on 10 July 1843 and it opened the following year with 40 beds. The area was then said to be 'a quiet place in an almost rural setting, remote from noisy streets and clamour of the market place – well out of the old walled town so that patients should have plenty of fresh air'. By 1971 it possessed 332 beds and that year treated no fewer than 8,000 in-patients and 173,000 outpatients. *(Bill Moore)*

The shop premises of Frederick Legge, Boot Manufacturer, 47 Foster Road, Bevois Valley, *c.*1905. *(Henry Brain Collection – Maureen Webber)*

The Antelope Hotel, 66 St Mary's Road, stands on the corner of Bellevue Street and dates back to the beginning of the 19th century. It closed in 1931 and the rear of the site is now occupied by the Charlotte Place roundabout. It was here that the Hampshire County Cricket Club was established in 1863, playing on the Antelope ground on the opposite side of the road. *(Bill White)*

'Dick' Lawrence with a customer, *c*.1925, serving in Cooper Brothers shop. Note the wealth of items on display. *(Margaret Wallace)*

'Dick' Lawrence, who rose in due course from Shop Assistant to Manager, proudly stands in the doorway of Cooper Brothers grocery and provisions shop at 136 Derby Road, on the corner with Durnford Road, *c*.1925. *(Margaret Wallace)*

By 1871 development had encompassed virtually the entire estate, with many of the properties designed for the more prosperous sections of the community. In that year Southampton Corporation compulsorily acquired land at St Denys for sewage disposal because drainage from the Portswood area was mainly into dead wells and the mud of the lower Bevois Valley. James Lemon (later Sir James), the Borough Surveyor, carried out massive improvements, incorporating a system of intermittent filtration that enabled the 25 acres of the Bevois Valley district to drain into the sewers of Mount Pleasant by gravitation. A further improvement came in 1884 when the practice of merely depositing the town's refuse in Bevois Valley was changed by Sir James into burning it, with the heat producing sufficient steam to pump the sewage.

a girl's school, a hostel for female Hartley University students, a World War One prisoner of war camp and a garage, was finally demolished in about 1940.

St Mary's Road, *c*.1920. The Co-operative Stores, opened in March 1907, are on the left, adjoining the Fire Brigade Station, with the Oxford Hotel in the background on the corner of St Mary's Road and Brintons Road. It then belonged to Barlow's Victoria Brewery, later changing to Brickwood's Brewery and now a Whitbread House. *(Joan Holt)*

The Territorial Army Drill Hall in St Mary's Road, Newtown, c.1910. Built in 1889, it was the headquarters of the 1st Hants Volunteer Artillery. The adjacent premises of G. Rice, 118 St Mary's Road, has a plaque marked 'Queensland Steam Bakery 1895' high on the wall and the premises continued to be used as such, by G. Fowler & Sons, Bakers & Pastrycooks, and subsequent bakers, until the late 20th century. It is now a very popular Leisure Centre. *(Dolly O'Beirne)*

By 1920 Bevois Valley had become a busy shopping area, with a number of small manufacturing premises such as the Winchester Brewery, a joinery factory and a small tobacco factory. The latter have since been replaced with more modern industrial premises.

The adjacent district of Newtown, to the south, was developed at the end of the 19th century with good quality semi-detached middle class homes in the Denzil and Cranbury Avenue area, and well-built terraced artisan homes to the east, leading down to the main railway line. One of the latter, Derby Road, was developed by 1875 on the line of an Anglo-Saxon road in Hamwic. Since World War Two this area has evolved, with an influx of immigrants, and now has its own special colourful character, adding to the richness of Southampton's diverse ethnic population.

The Newtown and Nicholstown sign at the top of Oxford Avenue. Based on a concept by Mark Ellison, it incorporates symbols representing the various ethnic communities in the area, together with doves of peace. Shipping is well represented, together with a typical terrace in the area and the tower block of Mount Pleasant School.

Further Reading

Local Studies Group, Southampton – *Portswood, Personal Reminiscences*, 1982.
Ticehurst Brian & Meachen, Harry *Pictures of Portswood's Past*, Kingsfisher Railway Productions, 1989.
Watson, Dorothy M. *Proud Heritage, History of the Royal South Hants Hospital 1838–1971*, G.F. Wilson & Co., 1979.

Bitterne

including Chessel

IT IS suggested that this name is derived from the Old English 'byhtaern', a building or storehouse by a bend, and this fits well with the prominent bend of the nearby River Itchen in the west. The modern Bitterne, however, is more associated with the immediate sur-rounds of Bitterne Village, on the crest of the high ridge bounded by Lances Hill in the west and the eastern edge of Bitterne Road.

Its earliest known origin is the small hamlet of work-ers' cottages erected by 1760 and called 'Bittern in Mousehole'. This arose out of increased farming in the area, coupled with a road leading to a new river crossing at Woodmill. This road appeared after the Itchen Navigation Canal was built in 1710 and residents no longer had to travel to the bridge at Mansbridge to reach Southampton. A track from Itchen Ferry, through Peartree en route to Woodmill, also entered the hamlet, and this, together with its access to South Stoneham Church, opened up the settlement for further expansion.

Southampton's prosperity as a flourishing spa in the mid-18th century gave rise to two reasons for the transition of the small hamlet of Bittern in Mousehole into the subsequent Bitterne Village.

One was an increased demand for farm pro-duce in the town and the area's ability to trans-port it via the new bridge at Woodmill. The other

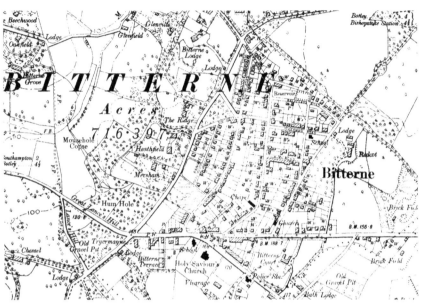

There were a number of grand country houses with spacious grounds to the west of West End Road in 1898, to the south of which was Great Lances Hill. The Chessel estate pos-sessed only one great house, built by David Lance, with one of its lodges shown at the top of what is now Chessel Avenue. Note the number of gravel pits and brickworks in the area. *(Reproduced from the 1898 Ordnance Survey map. NC/03/17894)*

was the attraction of this largely undeveloped area to the fashionable gentry, many of whom acquired land on the high ground on the eastern bank of the River Itchen to build their grand

Chessel House drive, leading from lower Chessel Avenue to the front of Chessel House, *c.*1910. The building, which stood approximately on the site of Nos 31 to 39 Chessel Avenue, was then uninhabited and awaiting development by Southampton Garden Suburbs Ltd. It was a favourite Sunday walk for local people and children and, as a sign of a different age, not a pane of glass in the house or large conservatory was broken until it was demolished in the mid-1920s. *(Bitterne Local History Society)*

Northam Bridge, c.1905. The first Northam Bridge was constructed of wood in 1799 and this wrought-iron bridge was built in 1889. The barrels have a white face because they were sealed with plaster-of-paris. They contained fat from the abattoirs of Paris, delivered three times a week for the nearby Northam margarine factory of Auguste Pellerine. *(Henry Brain Collection – Maureen Webber)*

houses. One good example of this is Chessel, at the south-west of Bitterne Parish.

The name Chesil, as in Chesil Beach, Dorset, means gravel or shingle, from the Old English 'ceosol', and is usually associated with a well-drained area. This may well have given rise to the Chessel name as the area's sloping contours down to the river Itchen certainly prevent it ever being water-logged! It directly adjoined the Roman supply base at Clausentum (the modern Bitterne Manor) and the Roman road leading eastwards to Chichester passed through it diagonally to reduce the steep incline.

There is no evidence of any significant occupation of this sloping area, known as Upper and Lower Guillames, until David Lance acquired it about 1790. He had served with the East India Company and was subsequently part of a financially successful partnership in China, returning to England in 1789 when he married and settled in Southampton.

In 1796 he built Chessel House on his estate, with attractive gardens commanding a fine view of the River Itchen and beyond to the New Forest. The initial steep portion of Bitterne Road adjoining the Chessel Estate was called Great Lance's Hill, joined near the top by a smaller road leading to Peartree called Lance's Hill, in deference to its developer. Their modern names have

Bitterne Church and School, c.1884. The 'Church of the Holy Saviour', to give it its correct title, was built in 1853 by William Gambling and served a Bitterne population of around 1,400. The first Vicar, the Revd Henry Usborne, and his sisters were the main contributors towards its cost. The picture was taken before the south aisle was added in 1887. The adjacent school was also financed by one of Revd Usborne's sisters. The family were renowned for their charitable deeds. *(Bitterne Local History Society)*

Bitterne Village, *c*.1909. On the right are Bitterne House (later called 'The Old House'); Bitterne Cottage (later 'Maytree') and 'Mon Repos', all now replaced by shops. The Red Lion public house is in the background, with the signpost showing the famous Y fork of the unsurfaced Bitterne and Bursledon Roads. *(Bitterne Local History Society)*

transposed to Lance's Hill and Little Lance's Hill (now a cul-de-sac) respectively.

At this time the only means of crossing the River Itchen to Southampton from the Chessel Estate was either by rowing boat at Itchen Ferry Village or the bridge at Woodmill. To overcome this inadequate access David Lance encouraged a move to build a bridge from Northam to Bitterne Manor, connected by a road giving a direct link to the east via Botley through Bitterne Village. This was well supported. Lance also backed a move to build a bridge over the River Hamble at Bursledon, approved by the Northam Bridge Company, with a new road leading to Portsmouth. By the end of 1799 the allied bridge companies had constructed both wooden toll bridges and the new roads. This gave rise to the famous Y-junction, or 'Bitterne Fork', where the Botley Road joined Bitterne Road. These new roads not only opened up considerable trade to the east but put an end to the comparative isolation of Bitterne Village. A subsequent Enclosure Act of 1812 enabled the local landowners to consolidate their estates and the area began to prosper.

In 1808 Jane Austen, then living in Southampton's Castle Square, wrote to her sister Cassandra about a visit to Chessel House, having gone there via the Itchen ferryman and returning over the new Northam Bridge. She described the house as 'a handsome building, stands high and in a very beautiful situation'. David Lance is thought to have died about 1819 and Lord Ashtown bought

Heathfield House was built in around 1830 and had a number of owners before becoming a private hotel in the 1930s. The stable block and staff quarters were converted into accommodation (still to be seen today in Montgomery Road) and a large bell on the north wall was used to call staff in from the grounds. By the end of World War Two it had become St Jude's Nursing Home but was demolished in late 1981. *(Bitterne Local History Society)*

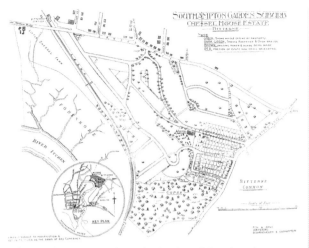

The 'Southampton Garden Suburb' plan of the Chessel House Estate, 1920. Chessel House and its three Lodges are shown. The alignments of Chessel Avenue, Chessel Crescent and Athelstan Road were subsequently changed and the two cul-de-sacs shown leading off the latter were not, in fact, built. *(Bitterne Local History Society)*

the estate about 1820. He was known as an enthusiast for converting the Irish peasants to the Protestant religion.

The remaining area of Bitterne Parish was developed in the early 1800s in two ways. The high area overlooking the Itchen valley was very desirable, as shown by the Chessel development, and this land was used for the building of large imposing homes, such as The Ridge, Mersham, Bittern Lodge, Heathfield, Moorlands and Brownlow.

These, in turn, required the services of workers and servants, and cottages were initially built in the Pound Street and Dean Road areas, rapidly extending to embrace the entire modern central Bitterne district. The original small cottages of Bittern in Mousehole were demolished as the local gentry extended their estates, and the impoverished tenants moved to the centre of the area.

Brickmaking was an important industry in Bitterne, as good quality clay was readily available where it came to the surface at the bottom and sides of the local hills, and this was an important factor in its housing development.

The 1830s thus saw the real growth of Bitterne Village, with the introduction of many small local shops, public houses and other amenities, and this expansion steadily continued. The original Red Lion public house was built in 1830 but the present well-known Red Lion Hotel, at the Bitterne Fork, was not built until 1862.

Spiritual needs were initially catered for in 1823 by a small Wesleyan Chapel in Dean Road (then Chapel Street). This was acquired by the Anglican Church in 1849 for a congregation of around 160, and replaced by the present large Church of the Holy Saviour, built nearby in 1853. The Wesleyans had built larger premises in Chapel Street in 1862, replaced by an even larger chapel in Pound Street in 1906. Education was catered for by a 'charity school' opened in Bitterne Grove in the 1840s and a number of private schools (five are shown in the 1851 census).

Communications further improved when Amos Rockett, a well-known local character, started his mail, omnibus and carrier service to Southampton in 1859, travelling twice daily via Northam to the railway terminus. At this period only the well-to-do had horses and carriages; most people walked to work, shop or just visit.

By the 1860s further large houses had been built in the immediate vicinity of the Village, including those in Bath Road, Spring Road, Freemantle Common and Lance's Hill, as an ever-

Chessel House Lodge, *c.*1900. Occupied by the Parker family for many years, this was one of the three Lodges leading to the Chessel estate. It stood at the junction of Lances Hill and Garfield Road and served as the laundry to Chessel House as well as the home of the toll collector. It was demolished in the mid-1950s. *(Bitterne Local History Society)*

increasing 'middle class' moved into the area, to eventually dispossess the gentry of their vast estates in the following century.

Chessel House had been purchased in 1840 by Sir William Richardson and was inherited by his eldest son, who died in 1906 and is remembered as a generous benefactor to the local poor. The house was then left uninhabited until 1910 when the estate was sold to Southampton Garden Suburb Ltd of Yeovil, who started building the Chessel Housing Estate in 1912. Most roads were laid out by 1913, although some plots were not auctioned and built on until after 1918. Houses were advertised for 'not more than £300 or £400.'

Of the three lodges to the estate only the modernised building on the corner of Chessel Avenue and Peartree Avenue remains. The other lodges, in Bitterne Road at the junction with Garfield Road and at the junction of Athelstan Road and Peartree Avenue, were demolished in the course of building development.

Bitterne became a civil parish under the Local Government Act of 1894, having previously been part of South Stoneham Parish. It then had a population of 2,253. (It had been less than 100 in 1800, when it included Bitterne Manor, Bitterne Park, Midanbury and Mousehole). The following

Landlord Steve Baker, with his father, is proudly standing in front of the John Barleycorn Public House, Commercial Street, c.1900. Named as though personalising malt liquor and often promoted to 'Sir', the premises date back to the early 1870s. It closed in 1983 and the Bitterne Health Centre was built on the site. *(Bitterne Local History Society)*

year, in 1895, Southampton Corporation proposed an extension to its boundaries to include Bitterne, a proposal that was vigorously resisted! However, in spite of strenuous efforts, the inexorable march of progress led to its incorporation into Southampton Borough in March 1920.

The economic recession after World War One, and the high cost of maintenance, resulted in many of the large estates following the example of Chessel and breaking up for residential development. New shops were built at the top of Lance's Hill and Bitterne Road and by 1921 the population had increased to 3,882. Bitterne rail-

Chessel Avenue, c.1930. The corner house on the right, No.2, was the home of Dr Alan Oakley-John, who set up a Christian General Practice there in 1948. When he retired, with his wife Gene, in 1978, they became missionaries with the Church Mission Society in Southern Sudan, ministering both medically and pastorally. They returned to Chessel Avenue in 1983 and he died in November 2000. The nearby Oakley-John Walk was named in his memory. *(Bitterne Local History Society)*

way station, opened in March 1866 at the bottom of Bullar Road, later served Woolston, Sholing, Netley and Fareham, to provide good communication with both Southampton and the east.

However, when Northam Bridge was purchased by Southampton Corporation in 1925 and its tolls freed in 1929, it caused great celebration in Bitterne. Bus routes to Southampton, West End and Woolston were immediately greatly improved. This complemented the electric tram service, extended in 1923 from Bitterne Park Triangle to the railway station, replaced by buses in May 1948.

The post-war period saw further dramatic changes to Bitterne. The remaining surrounding estates were sold for housing development, and the influx of residents changed the character of the former village. It became a busy suburb of an ever-expanding and thriving seaport. Large stores, branches of chain stores, banks, travel agents and the like replaced the small local family shops and tradesmen and the through traffic to and from the east increased as Southampton's trade developed.

Increased prosperity, with a consequent boost in car ownership, saw the traffic flow increase

The junction of High Street and Pound Street, *c.*1910. The corner building was originally the shop for Southwell's Dairy in nearby Dean Road but was bought by Lloyds Bank in 1915. The shop blind is outside Len Martin's, the shoe repairer. *(Bitterne Local History Society)*

The same view, 2004. Superdrug and Peacock's now occupy the entire frontage to the left of the bank.

Chapel Street, *c.*1905. So named because at various times there were three chapels in the road – Baptist/Anglican (now 75 Dean Road), Wesleyan (roughly on the site of the Sports Hall), and Congregational (on the corner with High Street). It was renamed Dean Road in 1924 following Bitterne's incorporation into Southampton. *(Bitterne Local History Society)*

Bitterne Road, *c*.1954, looking west, showing, centre to right, the Methodist Church at the bottom of Pound Street, then Bitterne Parade containing Bollom's Cleaners, Garrett's Chemists, Hayton Fruiterers, Lee Tobacconists, Glanvilles Hairdressers, Dewhurst Butchers and Hayton Florists. A portion of the Red Lion forecourt is on the left with the top of Lances Hill in the far distance. *(Bitterne Local History Society)*

The same view in 2004.

dramatically. The impact on the inhabitants was considerable and led to the most significant change to the village since it ceased to be Bittern in Mousehole – the massive Bitterne bypass, constructed in 1983.

A new dual carriageway cut a swathe through the north of the village, destroying many buildings and common land in the process. A landscaped shopping precinct and large car parks were created; a new swimming baths and sports complex built, with a new health centre nearby; and the Congregational (United Reformed) Church re-sited. The end result was a complete transformation of the old village, which no longer had to suffer horrendous traffic congestion, but risked losing its former character.

Looking east from the top of Lances Hill towards the Bitterne Fork in the early 1960s. The large 'Raleigh' sign on the left is above the well-known 'Sports' cycle shop on the corner of West End Road. A No.5 Corporation bus on the right is making its way towards town and the bell tower of the newly built 'Christ the King' Roman Catholic Church can be seen in the centre distance. *(Bitterne Local History Society)*

The same view in 2004, now fully pedestrianised.

Some old links remain – the horse trough at the top of Lance's Hill and the placing of the lion that had stood on the parapet of Lion Place onto a new pedestal in front of the Red Lion public house.

With the coming of the bypass members of the village community felt that its passing should not go unrecorded, and the Bitterne Local History Society was formed in 1981. Its collection of several thousand photos and artefacts, and its production of books and pamphlets dealing with its history, help keep alive the community spirit and old-fashioned values of the village that began as merely 'a bend in the river'.

Further Reading

Bitterne Local History Society *Bitterne – A Village Remembered,* Sholing Press, 1983.

—— *Bitterne Before the Bypass,* Sholing Press, 1991.

—— *Images of England, Bitterne,* Tempus Publishing, 1999.

Bitterne Parish Church *The Church with the Spire,* 2003.

Holt, John and Cole, Anne *A Bend In The River,* Bitterne Local History Society, 1992.

Marsh, Keith, *The Streets Around Bitterne,* 1996.

—— *Bitterne On The Map,* 1997, Bitterne Local History Society.

Pilson, Irene *Memories of Bitterne,* Kingfisher Railway Productions, 1984.

—— *More Memories of Bitterne,* Biddles Ltd, 1988.

Thompson, Eric *A Diary of Bitterne (Parts 1, 2 & 3 – 43 AD to 1959),* Bitterne Local History Society, 1996.

Wilkinson, Rosaleen *Bitterne School – A Diary 1862–1997,* R. Wilkinson, 1998.

Looking east in the late 1960s along Bitterne Road, with the Red Lion and Bitterne Fork in the background, to the left of the Church of the Holy Saviour. In the centre right is the Bitterne Bowl complex, in front of which is a much-reduced Sainsbury's store before it absorbed the site of the Angel Inn directly alongside. The houses in West End Road in the left foreground have been swept away and replaced by a parade of shops and Safeway store. Likewise, the houses in Peartree Gardens (now Angel Crescent) in the right foreground have been replaced by a car park and the relocated Bitterne School. *(Southern Daily Echo)*

Bitterne Manor

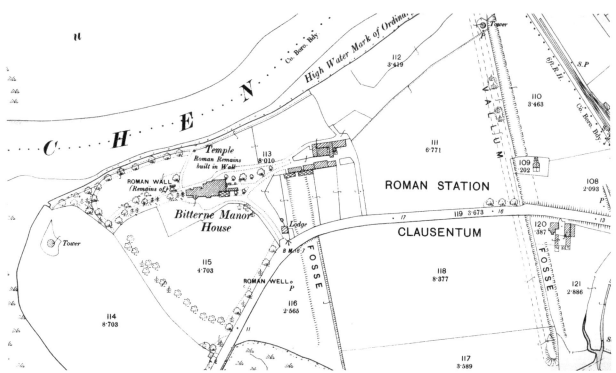

This 1897 map reveals the excavated evidence of Roman occupation by showing the traces of a Roman wall and well, and the fosse (otherwise moat). *(Reproduced from the 1897 Ordnance Survey map. NC/03/17894)*

BITTERNE MANOR takes its name from the later Middle Ages; it was then part of England's wealthiest see, granted by Edward I in 1294 to the Bishop of Winchester. He was one of the most powerful men in the kingdom and at the beginning of the 14th century his enormous estate consisted of nearly 60 manors and 10 boroughs, spread over the south of the country.

However, our first knowledge of the area comes from the Roman period, after the second invasion of Britain in AD 43. Southern Hampshire was garrisoned by the Second Legion, who made Winchester (Venta Belgarum) their local base.

By about AD 70 their supply base for the legions, at a sheltered peninsula on the River Itchen, had become an important trans-shipment port that local custom generally accepts as being the Roman 'Clausentum'. Its location, with its later double moats, made it more easily defended

from land attack and an ideal reception area for overseas imports. The modern Rampart Road, as its name implies, runs along the line of one of the defending moats and the rear gardens of the eastern side of the road can be seen to be sloping up.

However, some historians believe the site known as Clausentum to be elsewhere, arguing that the historical road measurements do not support a Southampton location. Be that as it may, this supply base was an important part of the road network that led to Winchester, Silchester and Chichester.

A Roman road book, published around AD 300, mentions a road to Winchester, Silchester and London (its precise line from within Southampton is not known) and 'Route 421', which led up the general area of the Chessel Estate to Peartree Avenue, en route to Porchester and Chichester. Part of this route has been traced from

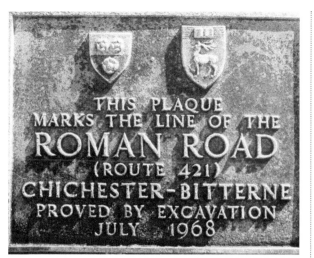

Plaque in Peartree Avenue at the corner of Freemantle Common, on the excavation point that proved the existence of the Bitterne to Chichester Roman road 'Route 421'.

Lady Macnaghten at Bitterne Manor house, c.1890. She was a forceful character and the family dominated the area for many decades. With her daughter Letitia she was a generous benefactor to local charities and the poor and occupied the leading position in local society. *(Bitterne Local History Society)*

1902 map of the Bitterne Manor Estate, as originally envisaged by the National Land Corporation after they had purchased it from Lady Macnaghten in 1895. The 'Roman Road' and the western part of 'Clausentum Avenue' were not built because the Macnaghten family repurchased the Manor House and its small surrounding plot. Clausentum Avenue was originally named Clausentum Road, but this was changed to Vespasian Road after the district was absorbed into Southampton in 1920, as there was already a Clausentum Road in Bevois Valley. *(Bitterne Local History Society)*

Freemantle Common to Sholing Common (on the former sports ground to the south of Bursledon Road), Weston Common and Netley Common.

There is no doubt that this local important Roman port was used to trans-ship goods arriving from abroad, but there is much conjecture as to which side of the river was used for storage and which side for garrison purposes. As if to answer this, the remains of a vast Roman building have now been discovered within the walled area of Clausentum, possibly a merchant's warehouse or more likely a military structure. It stood close to the water's edge on the tip of the peninsula.

As only one corner has been uncovered its full size is unknown, but it was at least 20m square. The excavated corner revealed 20cm square posts packed with Isle of Wight limestone, at intervals of five Roman feet, which had probably supported a substantial floor. The nature of the site and its type of structure are very similar to those at Fishbourne, where a military supply base is the generally accepted interpretation of the remains. There is also a strong body of belief that the British 'Emperor' Carausius established a mint at Clausentum but firm evidence of this has yet to be established.

Following the complete withdrawal of the Romans by the beginning of the fifth century, it is believed that Clausentum became a small early Saxon development, as a late fifth-century brooch and a number of apparent seventh and eighth-century burials have been discovered on the site.

Nothing is known of the area during the ensuing Dark Ages but the 14th-century Winchester Pipe Rolls (written manorial records) give details of the produce and livestock raised on the Manor, which then included much of the modern sur-

An unsurfaced Steuart Road, Bitterne Manor, c.1915. Developed in 1901, it runs from Bitterne Road West to Rampart Road and is now a cul-de-sac at its eastern end. (Bitterne Local History Society)

Bitterne Railway Station looking towards St Denys, c.1910. This was opened in March 1866 and the station building on the down platform enlarged in 1902. Until the present footbridge was erected in 1903 passengers had to cross the line on foot to get to the other platform! The station became unmanned in 1990 following the introduction of the electrical service. (Bitterne Local History Society)

rounding area of Bitterne and Bitterne Park. The cost of building repairs reveals something of the manor house and its outbuildings on the site of the former Clausentum. Earlier Pipe Rolls show that the Bitterne Manor building was a large farmhouse, with houses for its farm workers. It had 117 acres of arable land, consisting of 16 acres of wheat, 31 acres of barley and 70 acres of oats.

The Reeve of the Manor, mentioned in the Pipe Rolls, was its most important official, responsible for everything produced and consumed on the estate. He organised the work on the land and with the livestock, collected the rents, paid wages and was in overall charge of the estate. (The title 'Shire Reeve', of course, became corrupted to 'Sheriff') In 1302 this important official was a Walter le Parker, a well-known family name that persists in the area to this day. Is he possibly their ancestor?

Following the eventual decline of the manor at the end of the 16th century, most of the remaining Roman stone was removed and used for other buildings, such as Pear Tree church. A plan of the area drawn in 1804 shows only the Manor House, a barn, two large transverse ditches and the remains of Roman walls and banks. The Manor House, however, continued as a private residence and is shown on a map of 1791 as Bittern Farm. It is known that it became a hotel, the Bridge Tavern, following the construction of the nearby Northam Bridge in 1799, but by 1842 it had returned to its former name of Bitterne Manor House. Clearly, the tavern was not a commercial success.

The 1851 census has one of the earliest records of the family that was to dominate the district for many decades with its reference to Steuart Macnaghten, aged 36 and born in Madras. He was a barrister who was appointed Chairman of the Southampton Dock Company in 1869 and knighted by Queen Victoria in 1890. His Christian name and surname are frequently mis-

The Folly in Vespasian Road, *c*.1905. It is often mistakenly thought to be connected in some way with the Roman or mediaeval occupation of Bitterne Manor. The 1891 census records the residence of the Bailiff and his wife as 'Letitia Tower', named after Sir Steuart Macnaghten's daughter, and this almost certainly refers to this tower. *(Henry Brain Collection – Maureen Webber)*

spelt, but both can be seen in the roads named after him in today's Bitterne Manor.

Some indication of the status of Bitterne Manor House can be gleaned from the 1891 census. Sir Steuart was then aged 75, living with his third wife Amy, aged 49, and his two teenage daughters and son. Staff living in the house consisted of a Nurse/Housekeeper, Lady's Maid, Upper Housemaid, Cook, Schoolroom Maid, Kitchen Maid, Under Housemaid, First Footman and Under Footman. There were three buildings in the manor grounds: a Gardener's Cottage, with the Gardener and his wife; a Coachman's Cottage, with the Coachman and his wife, and, intriguingly, Letitia Tower (named after his daughter), where the Bailiff and his wife resided. The latter is thought to be the 'folly' still standing today in Vespasian Road.

Dramatic change came after Sir Steuart died in

1895. Four years later his widow sold the estate to the National Land Corporation, who were developing the adjacent Bitterne Park. The former extensive grounds of the estate were quickly developed, with the plots being sold by auction from 1902 onwards. However, Lady Macnaghten repurchased Bitterne Manor House in 1906, with seven acres of its surrounding ground, and her daughter, Miss Letitia, continued to live there until 1939.

The house was badly damaged by bombs in 1940 and left derelict for several years, until the well-known local architect, Herbert Collins, purchased it in 1950, for £2,150. He restored it as a block of 14 flats, as it remains today, set in its very pleasant private grounds, although the public still have access to part of the shoreline from Vespasian Road.

The Station Hotel on the corner of Macnaghten Road and Bullar Road, *c*.1890. It was allegedly built in 1880 as the property of the Cobden Bridge Brewery, but as the bridge was not constructed until 1883 this is most unlikely. Mr A.R. Powell, marked on the roof, was the first landlord and the adjacent clubhouse is still under construction. Henry Brain, thought to be the builder, lived less than 200 yards away and as Henry Brain Jnr., born 1871, took this photograph, the alleged earlier date is clearly incorrect. *(Henry Brain Collection – Maureen Webber)*

Further Reading

Brown, Jim *Bridging the Itchen*, Bitterne Local History Society, 2002.

Mann, John Edgar *The Story of Bitterne Park*, Ensign Publications, 1992.

Page, Mark *The Pipe Roll of the Bishopric of Winchester – 1301–2 and 1409–10*, Hampshire Record Series Vols XIV 1996 and XVI, 1999.

Williams, Robert *Herbert Collins 1885–1975*, Paul Cave Publications, 1985.

Bitterne Park

including Midanbury

The National Land Company's acquisition map of 1882 shows what is thought to be Middenbury House, just above the name Middenbury, with its Lodge (Middenbury Castle) at the junction of several roads to the north. There is a direct route leading from the Lodge to Townhill House. Note that Bitterne Manor Farm seems to consist of a substantial group of buildings. *(Southampton Archive Services Ref.SC/20/3/4/2)*

The front of St Mary's College in Midanbury Lane, *c.*1930. Formerly a country house called Bitterne Grove, it became the training centre for young Jesuit priests in 1910, exiled from France when anti-clerical laws were passed there in 1903. In 1922 it became the first Secondary School for Catholic boys in Southampton, under the name of St Mary's College, and opened with five Brothers and 30 pupils. *(Bitterne Local History Society)*

THIS district was, as its name implies, part of the parkland of Bitterne Manor, granted to the Bishop of Winchester in 1284. It was then surrounded by a high bank, with either hedging or wooden paling fencing on top, to protect the Bishop's cattle and sheep. (There is a record of several horses killed by wolves at nearby Hursley Manor during this period.) One of the first references to the park was in 1520, when Bishop Fox let 'the pasture called Bytterne Park' for 31 years to John Tanner, 'otherwise Mason of Weston', for an annual rent of £13 13s 4d. Tanner had to maintain all the walls, ditches, gates and so on.

By the end of the 18th century a few gentry estates had begun to appear on the outskirts of Southampton. Among these were Bitterne Grove and Middenbury House, to the east of the upper reaches of the River Itchen.

Bitterne Grove, now part of St Mary's College, was built about 1790 by Richard Leversuch but shortly after was purchased by James Dott. He was an eccentric and local legend says that the expression 'dotty' originates from him. When he died, in 1843, he left an endowment to West End Church of a length of red flannels for six parish widows. This endowment exists today, but is only worth about three pounds!

Middenbury House, believed to have been built by John Morse before 1791, was to the west

Midanbury Castle, c.1912. The Lodge to Midanbury House, showing its imposing castellated and turreted mock-Gothic gateway. It was demolished in the 1930s and the Castle Inn built on the site. *(Norman Gardiner Collection – Bitterne Local History Society)*

of Benhams Farm, somewhere between the modern Trent and Avon Roads. Its Lodge, also later known as Middenbury Castle, was at the junction of Woodmill Lane, Witts Hill and Midanbury Lane. This is one of the City's highest points and both the house and its lodge would have com-

manded a fine view across the surrounding countryside. The house has had many variations in the spelling of its name – ranging from its original Maidenbury to Midannbury and Middenbury. The modern name for the area, Midanbury, was never used with reference to the house, which had vanished by the 1930s.

Towards the end of the 19th century, apart from the above large estates, the only other dwellings in the immediate area were Bitterne Manor Farm to the north, close to Woodmill, and a few scattered cottages and brickfields to the east, beyond which was Benhams Farm. It is assumed that Bitterne Manor Farm was, in fact, the 'home farm', providing produce for the Manor House.

The area alongside the River Itchen, opposite St Denys, would therefore have presented a tranquil rural scene to those on the opposite bank, who would only have had fields and copses in

The original Cobden Free Bridge, c.1907. It was a 500-foot iron lattice girder bridge with five spans of over 70 feet, with 28 feet width between the centres of the main girders, which were six feet deep. The main supports were cast-iron cylinders seven foot in diameter, tested by running two traction engines with a combined weight of 20 tons across. The road was narrow by modern standards, only 16 feet, with six-foot pavements on either side. The old established family firm of Dyer's Boatyard can be seen on the St Denys side of the river.

Cobden Bridge, *c.*1995. By 1926 the increase in traffic on the bridge was such that a decision was taken to replace it with a new concrete one, but this took two years to complete. During this period a temporary wooden bridge was constructed alongside to provide continuity. The new bridge was officially opened on 25 October 1928 by Col. Wilfred Ashley, MP, the Minister for Transport, and was said to have cost £45,000.

Manor Farm Road, *c.*1902, with a Sunbeam Mabley, an unconventional vehicle that had a seat on each side facing in different directions. The wheels were in a diamond layout, with the front and back having offset single wheels and a wheel centrally at each side, belt driven by the exposed engine. This was a single cylinder 2.75hp, giving a top speed of 18mph and in 1901, when first produced, the car could be purchased for £130. *(Bitterne Local History Society)*

The Clock Tower in New Road, *c.*1900. Officially unveiled in December 1889, it was 'Bequeathed to the town of Southampton by the late Mrs Henrietta Bellender Sayers in evidence of her care both for man and beast'. It also bears the inscription 'Every beast of the forest is mine and the cattle upon a 1000 hills. Psalm L.10'. Over 43 feet high, the monument was designed by Sydney Kelway Pope and built by the local firm Garret & Haysom at a cost of £1,000. It has four dials and a drinking fountain with a trough for cattle and horses and at the foot, on the north and south sides, small troughs for dogs. The drinking fountain was on the west side and had a small cup suspended on a chain. *(Henry Brain Collection – Maureen Webber)*

view. However, this peace was rudely shattered, and the rural character of the area changed beyond recognition, when the National Liberal Land Company came upon the scene in 1882. This company had its origins in a wide spreading movement among working people who wished to own their own homes.

It purchased over 317 acres of this farmland from the Earl of Eldon for £26,415, with fields that stretched from Bitterne Station to Woodmill and up to Midanbury Lane. Some eight acres were reserved for a proposed cricket and lawn tennis ground and the remainder scheduled for extensive development, to be called the Bitterne Park Estate.

The company's advertising for the sale of freehold residential sites included the fact that 'It has a fine gravel soil and a gradually sloping and undulating elevation from the River Itchen, which skirts and bounds the Estate on the West, to a height of 200 feet. Extensive views of the New Forest, Netley and Southampton Water are obtained towards the south.'

This ideal vista was greatly enhanced by something that upset the shareholders of the tolled Northam Bridge – the provision of a free bridge! This would open up the district to west Southampton and was therefore a tremendous incentive for prospective purchasers. This did not mean that the Liberal Land Company was altogether altruistic; they had political objectives in mind. The right to vote was based on property qualifications and it was anticipated that the Estate would significantly boost the Liberal vote, as indeed it did.

The Clock Tower at the well-known Bitterne Park Triangle, c.1950. Henrietta Sayers's celebrated clock tower was moved here in 1934 from New Road in Southampton, and has now become the distinctive landmark of the district. Because of the soft soil on which it was built the clock tower is regarded as something of a local 'Leaning Tower of Pisa', as it tilts towards the adjacent Cobden Bridge by at least seven inches! It is on the triangular piece of ground where Alfred Chafen, the National Land Corporation's local agent, had his office in a wooden hut. Nearby Chafen Road, in Bitterne Manor, is, of course, named after him. (Bitterne Local History Society)

The Cobden Free Bridge, as it was called, was opened on 22 June 1883 and was crowded with a large number of dignitaries and spectators. The Chairman of the National Liberal Land Company, Professor J.E. Thorold Rogers, officially handed it over to the Mayor, Mr W.H. Davis, 'who accepted the gift amidst loud cheers.' Barriers were then removed and the party moved from the Southampton St Denys side of the river across to what was then the county area, where a large marquee had been erected for a luncheon.

Speeches, fully reported in great detail in the *Southampton Times*, placed much emphasis on the quality of the housing to be constructed on the new estate, especially the sanitation and water supply, and at a subsequent auction at the Dolphin Hotel plots of land were quickly snapped up, many of them fronting Bitterne Road for less than £100.

One of the first results of this splendid gift was

Macnaghten Road, c.1920. This was originally called Station Road and in 1901 was renamed in honour of the Macnaghten family, following Bitterne Manor's incorporation into Southampton Borough. The first small building-cum-shed on the left was the workshop of Sammy Griffin, a well-known deaf mute shoe repairer. Old Tauntonian Donald Finlay, international hurdler and captain of the British team in the 1936 Berlin Olympics, lived at No.115 as a young boy. (Bitterne Local History Society)

The Bitterne Park sign on the eastern side of Cobden Bridge. It shows a miniature clock tower, parkland vegetation and a swan. The latter are in abundance on this upper stretch of the River Itchen and are its distinctive feature.

named after John Bullar, the Chairman's former schoolmaster. Many of the new roads were named after Liberal supporters, such as William Cobbett, Sir William Harcourt and Joseph Whitworth.

Expansion of the Bitterne Park area continued at an ever-increasing rate, fulfilling the high hopes of the developers, now called the National Land Corporation, and generating more and more traffic to and from the Southampton side.

The Midanbury Estate, adjoining the initial development area, was sold to the local building firm T. Clark & Son in 1927 and they gradually developed the entire estate over the ensuing 20–30 years to the housing pattern of today. The mock-Gothic Middenbury Castle had become derelict in around 1935 and was demolished by 1939, when today's Castle Inn was built on the site.

The district of Bitterne Park, with its population of around 13,500, is now well developed with a character of its own and residents are fiercely proud of their full title, never, but never, to be confused with nearby Bitterne. Under no circumstances should one ever refer to the triangle of land at Cobden Bridge as 'Bitterne Triangle', without the inclusion of the essential word 'Park'!

somewhat surprising – resentment between the old Bitterne Village inhabitants and the people of St Denys, said to have originated when St Denys residents went primrose picking on the undeveloped estate. This resulted in the 'Battles of the Bridge', when gangs, armed with sticks and stones, would sally forth from either camp to wage war on the bridge itself. Battles of such ferocity ensued that the police had to intervene and the conflicts were eventually brought to an end. Bitter memories, however, were retained among the locals for many decades.

The name of Cobden came from the famous Corn Law abolitionist Richard Cobden, a relative of the Land Company Chairman, after whom Thorold Road was named. Bullar Road was

Further Reading

Brown, Doreen *The History of Bitterne Park Parish 1899–1999*, 1999.
Holt, John and Cole, Anne *A Bend In The River*, Bitterne Local History Society, 1992.
Mann, John Edgar *The Story of Bitterne Park*, Ensign Publications, 1992.

Southampton Docks

including Old (Eastern), New (Western) and Container Terminal

The laying of the foundation stone of Southampton Docks on 12 October 1838 by the Deputy Provincial Grand Master, Admiral Sir Lucias Curtis. The spire of St Michael's Church can just be seen to the right of the picture and God's House is clearly visible in the background. The stone was actually laid close by what eventually became No.1 Dock Gate, about 80 yards west of the site of the Docks Post Office, now a block of luxury apartments. *(Associated British Ports)*

ONE could be forgiven for expressing surprise at the notion of treating docks as suburbs, but Southampton Docks well satisfies the established criteria. In fact there have been three distinct dock 'suburbs': the Old or Eastern Docks, the New or Western Docks, and the Container Terminal – each reclaimed from the sea at different periods as a new development that extended the town.

Initially, in the 13th century, the port was centred on the West and Town Quays and its prosperity was based on importing wine and exporting wool. By the 15th century this had extended

The Outer Dock in 1889, before the opening of the Empress Dock by Queen Victoria the following year. Berthing space was obviously hard to come by at this time. The large twin-funnelled vessel in the centre background is the Peninsular and Oriental Steamship Navigation Company's *Arcadia*, somewhat different to the P&O cruise liner of that name today. To the left is the paddle steamer *Alice*, centre is the *Elbe* and right foreground the *Medway*. The gates of one of the earliest dry docks are in the foreground and barely seen in the background is the Royal Mail Steam Packet Company's workshops, later taken into use by Harland & Wolff ship repairers.

Troops of the Berks and Bucks Yeomanry returning from South Africa to a heroes' welcome at Southampton on board the P&O ship *Assaye* in 1900. The ship, built in 1899, was used for carrying troops during the Boer War and was broken up for scrap in 1928. *(Henry Brain Collection – Maureen Webber)*

to include trading in silks, spices and luxury goods from abroad. However, this diminished in the 16th century and by the early 18th century Southampton only enjoyed a coastal trade and links with the Channel Islands, as well as importing French wine. The quayside was then dry at low water and the town fell behind other ports that were improving their berths. Southampton's prosperity no longer depended on shipping but on its emergence as a fashionable spa. This, in turn, had declined by the early 19th century and the town's future was uncertain.

This changed dramatically in May 1836, when an Act of Parliament authorised the new Southampton Dock Company to construct a dock, the start of the 'Eastern Docks', on 216 acres of mudlands adjoining the Town Quay. The outcome of this venture, coupled with the formation of the London & South Western Railway in 1839, was to set the seal on Southampton's continued success up to the 21st century and beyond!

The first dock, constructed by 1842, was the Outer Dock, a tidal dock covering an area of 16 acres, and its first occupants were the 780-ton *Tagus* and the 450-ton *Liverpool*. They were both owned by the Peninsular & Oriental Steam Navigation Company, otherwise the celebrated 'P&O'. Although the line moved to London before the end of the century, it later returned and is still a major force in the port today. Another eminent line, the Royal Mail Steam Packet Company, formed in 1839, was also based in Southampton and continued to remain there for the ensuing 150 years. It had a Government contract for conveying the mail to and from Great Britain, the West Indies and the Americas and viewed Southampton as 'a Steam Boat Station unrivalled in England'. Rapid dock expansion followed – with a large Dry Dock constructed in

P&O maintain their troop-carrying tradition with the rust-streaked *Canberra*, seen on her return from the Falklands on 11 July 1982. The welcoming crowds, complete with banners, greatly outnumbered those that greeted troops returning from the Boer War and this photo shows only a fraction of the multitude that packed the quayside. However, *Canberra's* decks were as packed as that of the *Assaye* 82 years earlier.

The *Canberra* on her final return to Southampton on 30 September 1997, prior to going to the breaker's yard.

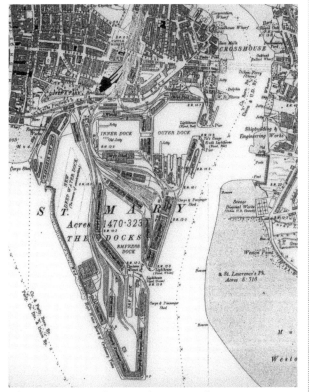

The 1911 Outer Dock is now the Ocean Village Marina complex and the Inner Dock has been filled in to provide office accommodation. The Empress Dock is still in use as Berths 20 to 27 but the remaining areas have been completely restructured as grain and ro-ro vehicle shipment terminals. *(Reproduced from the 1911 Ordnance Survey map. NC/03/17894)*

Prime Minister Clement Atlee opened the Ocean Terminal at 43/44 Berths in 1950. Built at a cost of £750,000, it was 1,297 feet long and 111 feet wide. It had a visitor's balcony that extended the length of the building, banking, customs and other facilities, and two fully self-contained large passenger lounges. Passengers had direct access to the ship by means of hydraulically operated telescopic gangways. It was demolished in 1983 and the area used for storing scrap metal.

1846, to receive the largest ship then built; an inner closed non-tidal dock by 1851, and two further Dry Docks by 1854.

The outbreak of the Crimean War that year saw Southampton firmly established as a major port, with the P&O Line alone transporting some 90,000 men and 18,000 horses. Another major shipping line, chartered for transporting stores at this time, also established an important link with Southampton – the Union Steam Ship Company. By 1900 this had become Union Castle, whose ships maintained a weekly mail service with South Africa, coupled with the import of fruit, until 1977.

1890 saw a major addition to the docks when Queen Victoria opened the 3,800ft quay Empress Dock. Southampton was then the only port in the country that could accommodate ships of the deepest draught at any state of the tide.

Two further dry docks followed, No. 5 Dry Dock in 1895 and Trafalgar Dock in 1905. However, increased trade, with the importance of Southampton for troop movements once again shown in 1899 on the outbreak of the Boer War, and the ever-improving road and rail connections, meant that the port again needed to expand. It had by this time passed into the ownership of the London & South Western Railway Company, who had loaned the capital for the construction of the Empress Dock. The White Star Line had also transferred their North Atlantic service here in 1907 and the increasing size of transatlantic liners demanded even more quay space. The White Star Dock was thus com-

The King George V Dry Dock in the course of construction in August 1932. Built as a joint venture by Howlem and Edmund Nuttell Sons & Co. (London) Ltd the project took two years to complete. It was the largest dry dock in the United Kingdom, 1,200 feet long and 135 feet wide at the entrance. *(Edmund Nuttall Ltd)*

pleted in 1911 and it was from Berth 44 in this dock that the ill-fated *Titanic* left on her uncompleted maiden voyage.

This increased quayside greatly assisted the demands placed on the port during World War One. This was a massive exercise in logistics, with over seven and a half million personnel, 850,000 horses, 175,000 vehicles, 14,500 weapons and three and a quarter million tons of stores and ammunition having passed though by 1919!

After the war the Cunard Steamship Company,

Creating the corner of 203/204 Berth in August 1971. The piles hold back the River Test prior to concrete being poured in to form the quay wall. British Telecom Marine Services initially used the reclaimed ground of 203 Berth for their UK Headquarters and as a base for their specialised cable-laying vessels. It has now become part of the container operation and the buildings demolished to provide additional stacking area.

turned to a large tract of land that had been purchased by the earlier railway company on the eastern side of the River Itchen before the war. This was dropped and Parliamentary approval was then sought and given to create a completely new docks complex, by reclaiming 400 acres of mudlands from the River Test between the Royal Pier and Millbrook Point. Thus began the port's next expansion and the creation of a new 'suburb' – the 'New Docks' self-contained docks estate.

In July 1928 the £13 million dock extension scheme got under way with 78 massive concrete

The newly formed 204 Berth in use by Solent Container Services in August 1972. Their first two cranes are still under construction and the small fleet of straddle carriers has only a handful of containers to handle. The stacking area is being created with concrete slabs, called 'stelcons', carefully laid on a bed of ballast to form an even surface.

another continuing valuable asset to the port, came to Southampton, and this was soon followed by a change of dock ownership. Sweeping changes to the structure of railway companies in 1923 resulted in the Southern Railway Company becoming the owners for the ensuing 25 years.

They quickly realised the pressing need to enlarge the dock capacity and thoughts initially

The post-war return of RMS Queen Elizabeth in the King George V Dry Dock c.1946. The dock sheds on Berths 101 to 108 have been completed and are in use, as is the massive Joseph Rank Flour Mill building. However, other familiar local industries, such as Martini Rossi, Standard Telephone & Cables and AC Delco, have yet to establish themselves on the available reclaimed ground. *(Edmund Nuttall Ltd)*

monoliths sunk into the bed of the River Test on behalf of Southern Railways. They were the start of 7,000 feet of deep-water quays running west from near the West Gate (where the *Mayflower* was moored in 1620) coupled with railway sidings, numerous sheds and a 1,200ft graving dock. This opened as the King George V Graving Dock in 1933. ('Graving' means to clean the bottom of a ship.) Local industries soon followed, and among the first was Joseph Rank's massive flourmill, opened in 1934 on 200 acres of reclaimed land adjacent to No.10 Dock Gate.

In 1939 Southampton Docks once again proved essential to the country in wartime and as such sustained a total of 69 air raids, causing much serious damage. However, early in 1943, with the invasion of France looming, the famous Mulberry Floating Harbour was constructed

Imperial House at 109 Berth, Western Docks, July 1971. This was the initial temporary home of Solent Container Services while the planning and construction of the nearby Container Terminal took place. In 1938 it was the Marine Air Terminal of Imperial Airways, whose four-engined flying boats carried mail and passengers to India, South Africa, the Far East and Australia, until it was suspended on the outbreak of World War Two. Imperial Airways became part of the British Overseas Airways Corporation (BOAC) in 1940, who then used 50 Berth in the Eastern Docks. BOAC left the port in 1950 and were followed by Aquila Airways, until they ceased operations in 1958.

Constructing the SCS workshop in 1972 to maintain the fleet of very tall specialised container-lifting straddle carriers and tugmasters. The latter towed the trailers used to transport containers to and from the nearby Freightliner Terminal.

The Container Terminal, c.1974. The ships on 201/202 Common User Berths in the background are being handled by BTDB staff and the GPO Cable Depot has yet to be constructed on 203 Berth at the corner. The two first-generation container ships on 204/205 Solent Container Services berths at the right would now be considered small. They have containers three high and 10 across on the deck, compared with the modern six high and 20 across. There are only three Portainer cranes on the SCS berths, compared with the current 13 far larger versions, and the general stacking area is less than a quarter of that today. (Associated British Ports)

year it was decided to build a new Ocean Terminal worthy of these great ships. Legislation also brought about a change of dock ownership and by 1953 it had become the British Transport Docks Board (BTDB) docks. More large industrial sites became established in the Western Docks, with Standard Telephone & Cables in 1954, the International Cold Store in 1956, AC Delco and a wine plant, the forerunner of the Martini Rossi bulk storage and bottling wine depot, by 1965.

The visit of HRH Prince Charles on 10 April 1985. The author, standing on right, recalls with some amusement being informed that a militant individual had refused to move his car from a no-parking security area where the Prince was going to walk. The person was told, 'Great! I've never seen a car boot blown open and the bomb squad will be here any minute'. The car was moved immediately.

However, by the early 1960s cruising was being replaced by the quicker jumbo jets and the shipping lines saw a reduction in the number of passengers. The port authorities took this in their stride and turned to fresh fields to conquer – cargo containerisation and ro-ro traffic (roll-on/roll-off of vehicles into specially adapted vessels). The latter were increasingly handled in the New Docks as the liner trade was reduced, but the former required large areas of container stacking space.

Thus, in 1967, the construction began of the third dock 'suburb', an extension of the New Docks (now called the Western Docks) with new quays between the King George V Graving Dock and Redbridge.

within the docks, under a veil of secrecy, and later floated across the Channel as part of Operation Overlord. The port was also completely saturated with landing craft, troops and equipment prior to D-Day and the success of the military operation can be partially credited to civilian port staff. (The return of Canberra and the QE2 from the Falklands in 1982 was yet another example of the port's useful role in military operations.)

The end of the war brought cruising back to the port, with the return of the Queen Mary and Queen Elizabeth in August 1945. The following

A Portainer crane under construction on newly reclaimed 207 Berth in 1968. When finally assembled these 800-ton machines were moved 400 yards on a platform of wheeled bogeys that hydraulically lifted the massive frame above the ground. They were then pushed by lorries, at a walking pace, and carefully inched into place onto the quayside rails.

The initial Berth 201 was used as a Common User Berth, with Dart Line and Seatrain container ships handled by dock staff, but in July 1971 a new independent organisation came to Southampton, Solent Container Services, setting the seal on the terminal's future. (The author joined the company at this advanced planning stage as their Chief Security Officer).

Originally housed in temporary accommodation in Imperial House at 109 Berth, SCS was to handle the Far East container traffic for an international consortium, TRIO, composed of major British, German and Japanese shipping lines, with a total of 17 large container ships. An additional 3,900 feet of quayside had started in June 1970 but their first ship, the NYK *Kamakura Maru* was handled at the newly constructed 202 Berth on 29 January 1972. Berth 204 came into use that June, linked to a new large Marine Freightliner Terminal to its north, and since that time the terminal has seen consistent and steady growth, expanding into further international trades with South Africa and China. The quayside has been ever-expanding and is currently 4,430 feet long, extending from their original 204 Berth to 207 Berth.

Now called Southampton Container Terminals Ltd, owned jointly by ABP (BTDB changed to Associated British Ports in 1982) and P&O, the massive operation handles around one and a half million container units annually on its 180 acres of stacking area. As many as 22,000 units have been handled in a single week, and four of the largest container ships in the world can be dealt with simultaneously. These latest container ships, of around 100,000 gross tons and 1,056 feet long, have the capacity to carry over 8,000 container units and require specialised facilities for loading and unloading.

The Southampton Container Terminal therefore has state-of-the-art computerised equipment and modern systems technology unrivalled anywhere in the country. Some of its 13 massive gantry cranes have a 66-ton lift capacity and can handle ships that have containers stowed 20 wide. It also has 94 straddle carriers, 28 of which can handle containers stacked four high, including two with twin-lifters, and 66 can handle

A 2004 view of a section of the Southampton Container Terminal on the River Test, taken from the western end of 207 Berth and looking towards the Western Docks. When the fourth massive container ship is finally moored alongside, all four berths will be occupied and several thousand import and export containers will be handled in a matter of hours. *(Southampton Container Terminals Ltd)*

three-high stacks, including 41 twin-lifters. The operation is computer controlled, with the computer allocating stack positions to the straddle carriers, whose precise location can be pinpointed by a global satellite positioning system. It is a far cry from the manual handling of cargo in the past by hundreds of dockworkers.

The Old Docks continues to play its part, heavily involved in ro-ro traffic and grain silos, but with housing and business development replacing the outdated cargo handling areas. The popular Ocean Village, currently being extensively remodelled, is the original first Outer Dock, constructed in 1842, and is now a prestige yacht marina.

The port of Southampton, therefore, with its three distinct areas of reclaimed land, continues to be one of the country's leading ports and an integral part of the City's economy. This was established beyond doubt with the arrival of the massive *Queen Mary 2* in Southampton on Boxing Day 2003. This, the largest cruise liner in the world, owned by the American Carnival Corporation (owners of both P&O and Cunard) has made Southampton its UK home port, and confirmed the port's prestigious status.

The largest passenger liner in the world, the 150,000-ton *Queen Mary 2*, sailing into her home port of Southampton on Boxing Day 2003. With a length of 1,131 feet, 131 feet width and costing £550 million, she can carry 1,253 crew and 3,090 passengers. *(Jonathan Bunn)*

Further Reading

Arnott, Alastair *Maritime Southampton* Breedon Books, 2002.

Hawes, Duncan *Cunard, Triumph of a Great Tradition* Cunard, 1990.

Hovey, John *A Tale of Two Ports* The Industrial Society, 1990.

Howarth, David & Stephen *The Story of P&O*, Weidenfeld & Nicolson, 1994.

Hyslop, Donald; Forsyth, Alastair & Jemima, Sheila *Titanic Voices,* Southampton City Council, 1994.

Leonard, Alan and Baker, Rodney *A Maritime History of Southampton in Picture Postcards,* Ensign Publications, 1989.

Moody, Bert *150 Years of Southampton Docks,* Kingfisher Railway Productions, 1988.

Williams, David, *Docks and Ports: 1 – Southampton,* Ian Allan, 1984.

Harefield

IN THE 12th century this area was mainly open common land and part of the Abbot of Netley's Manor of Townhill. By 1806 it had become agricultural land with a farm called Newlands located roughly where Beauworth Avenue now joins West End Road.

Its first real development came in around 1846, when Harefield House was built for Sir Edward Butler, former Chairman of the Southampton and Salisbury Railway Company. The reason for the choice of name is unknown. It could have come from a field with a large colony of hares or unrecorded tenants by the name of Hare, but this is pure conjecture.

The mansion was impressive. All the main rooms had 12ft 6in high ceilings and the 29ft x 18ft dining room led directly into a 40ft x 20ft conservatory. There was an arboretum, ornamental pool, terraced gardens, tennis courts, large kitchen garden, stables and two stone summerhouses. It also had double and single coach houses, with a three-stall stable, and accommodation for a groom and his family. There was a brick-built riding school, measuring 60ft by 30ft, a peacock aviary, icehouse and two substantial lodges, both of which were along what is now West End Road. There were also a number of cottages occupied by various staff, one of which, 21 Balaclava Road, still stands.

The estate was described as beautifully undu-

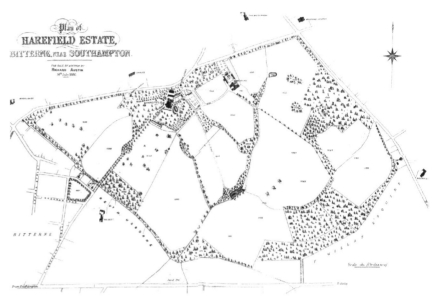

Map of the Harefield estate when sold by auction on 14 July 1886. It shows the open nature of the estate, with the adjacent Moorlands to the northwest and Shales to the north. Redcote lies in the south, with Balaclava, Inkerman and Alma Roads to its west. Note the large 'pheasantry' area to the east. *(Bitterne Local History Society)*

lating and was divided into enclosures of pastureland and numerous belts of trees, many of which are still visible today. The arable land was well cultivated and had a number of pools, including a fishpond and a large pond with an island.

The walled garden (at the junction of the mod-

Harefield House, *c*.1915. (It stood between Nos 143 and 153 Yeovil Chase.) The 1886 sale document states that 'The mansion is a most substantial erection of the Elizabethan-style architecture, standing on an eminence approached from the main road by three entrances, by winding carriage drives leading to a bold porte-cochere entrance. On the summit is an observatory with a revolving dome, fitted with divisional openings, with store room beneath.' *(Bitterne Local History Society)*

Harefield House coachmen Mr Thomas and Mr Morant at their stables, *c*.1910. The number of servants in the household in the 1891 census shows Edwin Jones's status. Living in the house or lodge were a butler, cook, two housemaids, kitchen maid, general domestic, coachman, groom, two gardeners and a bricklayer, as well as a number of general labourers living in estate cottages. *(Bitterne Local History Society)*

vegetable garden and two orchards. When, after several owners, the 238-acre estate was offered for sale in 1886 it was described as 'a most attractive and compact freehold residential and sporting estate'. By this time the Newlands farm had been renamed Homestead. It had three cottages, a dairy, and an enclosed yard that contained stabling for eight horses, eight cow stalls and nag stables with four loose boxes. It also included three poultry houses, two piggeries each with five pens, a slaughterhouse, carpenter's shop and a double-bay barn. Altogether a most substantial farm!

Edwin Jones purchased the estate in 1889 and he is the person most associated with it. He was an astute businessman, with imposing premises in Southampton's East Street. Initially a small haberdashery shop, rented with his two sisters, it became one of Southampton's principal stores, due to his capacity for hard work coupled with resourceful dealing in cotton during the American Civil War. He was Mayor of Southampton twice,

ern Melchet Road, Selborne Avenue and Yeovil Chase) was equally impressive and sufficiently productive to cater for the large household. There was a 150ft run of vineries and orchard houses, with peaches, apricots, blackberries, raspberries and quinces, as well as a 50ft by 16ft heated plant house. Outside of the walled garden were a large

Shales, West End Road, *c*.1884. It was occupied by Sir Charles Coote from about 1850 and sold to his brother, Admiral Robert Coote, in 1865. Demolished around 1970, St Francis House and St Theresa House (sheltered accommodation) were later built on the site. *(Bitterne Local History Society)*

Harefield show bungalow in August 1960, after severe flooding in the valley between Bitterne and Thornhill. The bungalow, No.6 Somerset Avenue, was built by Somerset Gardens Estate Ltd in 1938. Work on the estate ceased on the outbreak of war but was resumed by Southampton Corporation before they took the area into the borough in 1954. *(Bitterne Local History Society)*

in 1873 and 1875, and played a leading part in many of the town's political and social activities. At the time of his death he was also the Deputy Lord Lieutenant of Hampshire.

Edwin Jones died in 1896 and was buried in West End cemetery. Although his widow remarried she continued the hospitality that had always been shown to the local inhabitants by her former husband. She was widowed again in 1913 when her husband, Dr Thomas, died of blood poisoning after injuring himself while pruning roses.

Disaster struck Harefield House at about 8.20am on Sunday 6 May 1917 when the family were at Holy Communion at West End Church. (Not, as mistakenly recorded in some local publications, on 4 April 1915) It is thought that sparks from the kitchen chimney ignited some leaves caught on the roof, and the resultant fire spread rapidly. By the time the fire brigade arrived at 9.00am the flames had enveloped the roof, helped by a strong wind, and the house could not be saved. Nothing remained except the exterior walls. A crucial factor that hindered the fire brigade was an inadequate supply of water due to a newly opened RASC Remount Depot at Swaythling also placing a demand on it. This was where soldiers in transit could exchange their horses while on a journey. The incident gave rise to the now famous remark of Captain Sillence, the officer in charge of the fire brigade, who said, 'Well, I could piddle faster than that!'

As a result of this calamity Mrs Thomas placed the entire estate on the market that November. It included the farm, which had reverted to the name Newlands, and now had a terrace of three houses. In the event, Mrs Thomas conveyed the entire estate to Edwin Jones & Co. Ltd that December, no doubt in recognition of the contribution played by its 1,200 staff in the development of the estate.

The company made the most of this wonderful acquisition and created the remarkable 'Edwin Jones Staff Recreation Ground'. The riding school was converted into a pavilion, with changing rooms, canteens for light meals and teas and it was later also used for dances. Fields were made into hockey and football pitches, tennis and netball courts were laid out, together with a first-class cricket pitch. Stables were also converted into accommodation for a resident groundsman and his family. The facilities were not restricted to staff of Edwin Jones & Co. Ltd, but were also made available to local residents for festivities and celebrations. The company also had a tenancy agreement with the farm, which supplied the Southampton store with much of its produce.

1928 brought changes to the area, starting with the absorption of the company, then part of the Drapery Trust Ltd, into Debenhams Ltd. This coincided with land development at the western edge of the estate, when Hatley and Wynter Roads were built. An attraction for incomers was the belief that the vast adjoining sports ground would never be built on and that it would remain an open space. Land values in the area were inflated as Southampton's needs grew and by 1934 the Board of Edwin Jones was actively considering the development of the estate. Various offers were received and rejected, but in November 1935 it was agreed to construct a new eight-acre smaller sports complex close to West End Road and to develop the remainder. These new sports facilities only continued for a few years, as by 1939 falling membership and financial problems resulted in closure. (The site was eventually sold to Southampton Corporation, who built the modern Harefield Infants and Junior schools on the site in 1951.)

Development was started in the late 1930s by Somerset Gardens Estates Ltd, who first built a main road through the estate along an existing farm track in the valley. They called it Somerset Avenue and all their subsequent roads were named after Somerset towns or villages. At this time it was assumed that the Edwin Jones' Sports ground, between Yeovil Chase and West End Road, would remain. However, World War Two meant that their plans could not be fully realised and a shortage of materials and manpower brought the development to an end.

The construction of the present large council estate resumed in the early 1950s, before Harefield was taken into the borough in 1954, but the road layout was different to that planned and roads were named after Hampshire villages. There have been many changes since then. The planned churches were not built; two schools that were built have been demolished; more shops have been added and many houses are now privately owned. Harefield currently has a population of around 13,000, living in one of the most pleasant of Southampton's outlying suburbs.

Further Reading

Bitterne Local History Society *Images of England – Bitterne*, Tempus Publishing, 1999.
Marsh, Keith *Harefield, A Hidden Heritage,* Woodlands Community School, 1999.

Highfield

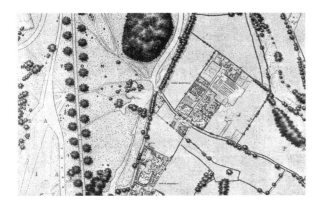

1845 map of Highfield. The scale of the map is such that the house names are not legible, but an 18th-century mansion, 'Hayfield Villa', is shown in 'Upper Highfield'. Its large brick-field, kiln and gardens are next to the Rose and Crown public house (closed in the 1880s) on the corner of Highfield Lane and Highcrown Street (then called Crown Street). Further south, at the top of Oakmount Avenue, is the imposing reputedly Georgian mansion, Highfield House, of which only the lodge house still stands. 'Highfield Villa' is in the named 'Lower Highfield', with its spacious and well laid out gardens on the site of the 20th-century Taunton's School, now the Southampton University Avenue Campus. *(Reproduced from the 1845 Ordnance Survey map. NC/03/17894)*

HIGHFIELD lies in the north-west section of the parish of Portswood and bears an obvious and self-explanatory name, confirmed by an 1845 map of the area that shows large hedged fields on the high ground to the east, bounded by the Common and The Avenue to the west. It shows Highfield Villa, Hayfield Villa and Highfield House and the district was otherwise sparsely populated, with a scattering of small cottages and a single line of semi-detached houses with long

Christ Church pre-1914, on the corner of Highfield Lane and Church Lane, formerly called Portswood Back Lane. The winding lane has not changed materially since that time, but now leads to the massive University complex. *(Norman Gardiner Collection – Bitterne Local History Society)*

'Oakdene', Welbeck Avenue, Highfield, the home of Sir Sidney Kimber. A Tory leader and Mayor in World War One, he earned his knighthood in 1935 by, among other attributes, forcing through his visionary realisation of the town's excellent Civic Centre and outstanding Sports Centre. They continue as lasting and worthwhile amenities for the City. He was also responsible for the widening of Highfield Lane and the installation of gas lighting in Portswood. *(Norman Gardiner Collection – Bitterne Local History Society)*

A very rare view of the interior of the Hartley University College in Southampton High Street, c.1910. This opened in 1862 as the Hartley Institution out of a bequest in the will of Henry Robinson Hartley, an 'eccentric scholar naturalist'. Numerous glass-covered trays of exhibits can be seen on the lower floors, and there are packed bookshelves on the top floor. Animal horn trophies and shields, including one of the Southampton red and white roses emblem, decorate the walls. *(Norman Gardiner Collection – Bitterne Local History Society)*

gardens in Highcrown Street. A hint of Highfield's future significance to the town, however, is revealed by a small school near the Good Intent public house, to the east of Hayfield Villa. It was an indication of the shape of things to come.

Up to 1847 the church of St Mary in South Stoneham had served the needs of the surrounding area, including Highfield, but the ever-increasing population of Portswood demanded a more convenient place of worship. Thus, on 17 September 1847, the consecration of Christ Church took place. Highfield Church Day School, built at the rear of the church, followed in 1849. This was a National School, teaching the children strong moral values, and by 1890 it had 304 pupils. A further strengthening of the district's educational resources occurred in 1904 with the opening of Portswood School, to accommodate 360 boys, 360 girls and 400 infants. The area had by then developed into a select area,

Taunton's School, Highfield, c.1950. It ceased to be a Grammar School in 1967 and, after a transitional period, became a Comprehensive Secondary College for sixth form pupils in 1971. Further blows to Taunton's traditionalists followed when the College became co-educational in 1978 and in 1993, when it was relocated in the former Girls' Grammar School buildings in Hill Lane, officially opened the following January by an Old Tauntonian, Lord Clive Hollick. The school has a number of famous ex-pupils, including Benny Hill; Donald Finlay (captain of the British Olympic team 1936); Ken Russell; John Stonehouse and Southampton's only holders of the Victoria Cross in two world wars, Daniel Beak and Jack Mantle. Dr Horace King, later Lord Maybray King, Speaker of the House of Commons, was the school's English Master from 1922 to 1947 and taught the author. *(Norman Gardiner Collection – Bitterne Local History Society)*

Aerial view of the University War Hospital and hut wards before their demolition, c.1926. The Medical Officer of Health for Southampton, Col. R.E. Lauder, took command of the Hartley University College's new home in 1915 as an emergency hospital and it was staffed by nurses from the British Red Cross Society. The horrific toll of casualties arriving from France soon meant that large wooden huts had to be erected at the rear of the 'hospital' to serve as additional wards. *(Norman Gardiner Collection – Bitterne Local History Society)*

University Road on the occasion of the visit of HRH the Prince of Wales to the University on 27 June 1924. The Stile Inn on the right, at the corner of Burgess Road, was destroyed in an arson attack in 1990. It has since been replaced by modern premises and continues to cater for the large number of students in the area. *(Norman Gardiner Collection – Bitterne Local History Society)*

Shaftsbury Avenue, at the junction with Highfield Lane and leading to Welbeck Avenue, *c.*1930. The horse and cart plodding up the hill are typical of those delivering such commodities as bread, coal, groceries and milk before the advert of the modern supermarket. The first property in this road, recorded in 1900, was Shaftsbury House, occupied by Mrs Bushell, but others soon followed. *(Norman Gardiner Collection – Bitterne Local History Society)*

with many good detached houses owned by the gentry, army officers, an Admiral and wealthy businessmen.

One such wealthy family were the McCalmonts, who came from Ireland and settled in Lower Highfield, just north of Highfield Cottage, calling their estate 'Uplands'. Another notable family were the Kimbers. Richard, a schoolmaster, had purchased the brickfield north of Hayfield Villa. It was his son Sidney, however, who made the name outstanding locally. He had started work at the age of 14 in his father's brickworks, and after taking it over from his father ran it until the clay was exhausted in 1935.

On 20 May 1914 the Hartley University College moved to Highfield, into new buildings constructed in Back Lane (now University Road). This was the beginning of the complete transformation of the area, massively increasing its strong emphasis on educational resources and a move that continues to have repercussions to this day. However, before the move could take place

World War One began and the newly constructed buildings were commandeered as a Military Hospital. It was not until 1919 that the University staff and students could take up occupation and wooden huts were used for student training for some years, until demolished to make way for permanent brick buildings.

By 1926 Highfield's population was estimated to have doubled to 8,000 over five years and in the poorer areas there were still five-roomed cottages with 15 occupants. It was, however, starting to lose its 'upstairs/downstairs' image.

Another significant event occurred in Highfield in 1925 when Taunton's School, with 600 pupils, moved there from its New Road premises in the town.

Alderman Richard Taunton, a wealthy wine merchant who died in 1752, left many legacies in his will with the remainder devoted to '... the employment and maintenance of Poor People there [in Southampton] and bringing up their children in Work and Industry fitting them for the

Furzedown Road, leading off Highfield Avenue, *c.*1909. A small group of children pose for the photographer outside the small private St Nicholas School, one of many in the neighbourhood. The road first appeared in local directories in 1900, with one house, but was quickly developed. *(Bill Moore)*

sea.' After some dispute this eventually resulted, in 1760, in a small Foundation school for 'not more than 20 boys' who were later to be apprenticed to the sea. By 1864 it had developed so well that purpose-built premises were opened in New Road with about 50 pupils and in 1875 it became Taunton's Trade School, a title that lasted until

This welcoming sign in Highfield Lane has Christ Church, in the heart of the district, as its theme.

1907 when it became a public secondary school. By 1924 the numbers had increased to about 500 and the New Road premises proved inadequate.

Early in 1913 the Chairman of Governors, William Spranger, had purchased the five-acre site known as Highfield Uplands (in the grounds of the former Highfield Villa) between The Common and Heatherdene Road. World War One disrupted plans to build a new school on this site and it was not until 5 March 1925 that the foundation stone was laid and the staff and pupils moved in the following year. By 1933 there were 800 boys and 36 masters and the school had a good and improving reputation. The pupils and staff spent the World War Two years evacuated to Bournemouth, during which time the Highfield buildings suffered from occupation by troops, prisoners of war and air raids, but this was rectified after the school returned in September 1945. The buildings were taken over by Southampton University as the Avenue Campus when the college relocated to Hill Lane in 1993 and remains as such today.

An interesting link between the University and Taunton's is the fact that George Robinson, a wine importer who rented some of Taunton's vaults, helped Alderman Taunton's widow in the management of her affairs. It was his nephew,

Henry Hartley, who made the fortune inherited by Henry Robinson Hartley, founder of the Hartley Institute that became Southampton University.

In 1952 the University College at Highfield became, by Royal Charter, the University of Southampton, with a total number of students of just under 1,000. By 1967 this had grown to over 4,000 and the Sir Basil Spence Partnership drew up a master plan for the development of the 32-acre site. This included the design and layout of the sloping gardens in the west of the site, around which are grouped the Faculty of Science buildings and the locally very popular Nuffield Theatre, seating 500, assisted by a grant from the Nuffield Foundation.

The modern Southampton University has now expanded tremendously, not only on the Highfield site but also with campuses and buildings throughout the City. It has well over 20,000 students within its eight faculties, all of which enjoy an international reputation, and it now ranks among the top British universities.

A further distinctive aspect of Highfield is the Uplands Estate, designed by Herbert Collins in the 1920s–30s. His obituary in 1975, by the former City Architect, Leon Berger, paid him the tribute of being 'the most important architect in the housing field that Southampton has even seen'. His estates are a distinctive feature of Southampton's suburbs and are skilfully arranged in informal settings around well-preserved features of the original topography. Most were two-storey houses in a basic Georgian style, with low-pitched roofs, built in small terraces arranged around a small green or along grass-bordered roads, retaining the original trees. His first Southampton estate was the remaining 19 acres of Uplands that he purchased in 1923. Over the ensuing 20 years he built over 200 houses and flats, all in his distinctive style, either leased for 999 years or privately let.

Highfield's reputation as a centre of educational excellence has been established over the years by not only the several schools already mentioned, but also by many former 19th-century private schools in the area. This concentration of educational establishments, as well as the fine University, has given Highfield a well-deserved scholastic reputation, which remains to this day.

Further Reading

Anderson, Alexander *Hartleyana – Henry Robinson Hartley,* Southampton University Press, 1987.

Gardiner, Norman *The University of Southampton as a War Hospital,* Kingfisher Railway Productions, 1983.

Kimber, Sir Sidney *Thirty-eight Years of Public Life in Southampton 1910–1948,* Privately published, 1949.

Mann, John Edgar and Ashton, Peter *Highfield, A Village Remembered,* Halsgrove, 1998.

Patterson, A. Temple, *The University of Southampton,* Southampton Press, 1962.

Reader, Elizabeth, *Highfield Church, 1847–1997,* E. Reader, 1998.

Spooner, H. *A History of Taunton's School 1760–1967,* Camelot Press, 1968.

Williams, Robert *Herbert Collins 1885–1975,* Paul Cave Publications, 1985.

Maybush

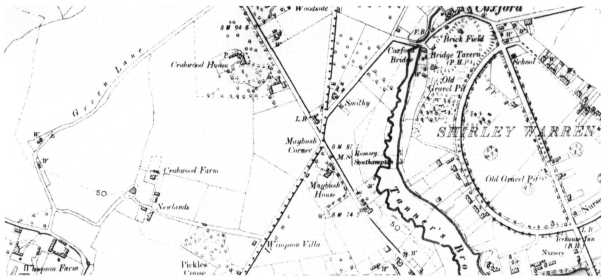

This 1898 map of the Maybush area shows its then absolute rural character. Crabwood House and its neighbouring farm dominate the scene, that otherwise consists of fields and a scattering of small country houses. Two essential businesses are marked – a smithy just north of Maybush Corner and the Bridge Tavern, near the road bridge over Tanner's Brook in Coxford. *(Reproduced from the 1898 Ordnance Survey map. NC/03/17894)*

THE earliest known settlement in this area is from the Iron Age, with traces of habitation dating between 300 and 50 BC found at the corner of Romsey Road and Green Lane, near Millbrook Community School. Archaeologists believe it was a farmstead supporting between 30 and 40 people, possibly an extended family group. No trace of further occupation was found beyond 50 BC and it is probable that the farmland became unproductive, leaving the fields to become pasture.

It is uncertain as to whether the area of Maybush was within the Anglo-Saxon Manor of Millbrook or that of Nursling, but on balance it is thought to be within Nursling. The boundaries outlined in the land charter of 956 seem to place Maybush just outside the north-west corner of Millbrook Manor, which appears to have been a scattering of small farms.

Charles Marrett, the owner of a shipyard near Westgate House, his Southampton home, built Crabwood House, Maybush in the 1840s for his sister, Frances. It was on the west of Romsey Road

near Maybush Corner, and was purchased in 1852 by Rolles Driver, a 'foreign timber and slate merchant', who lived there until about 1877. The later 1899 *Directory* shows a total of 10 families living in Maybush, a shoeing smith, baker, cattle dealer and three market gardeners, who probably occupied most of the land. The tenant of Crabwood House was then Horatio Smith.

The house and 230 acres were sold to the Claremont Estate Company in 1936, who in turn sold the house and immediate grounds to the Ordnance Survey Office in 1938. The building was the Ordnance Survey Sports & Social Club for many years, but in 2003 the OS decided that it could no longer afford to maintain the internal fabric of the building and the club's tenancy was terminated. However, the structure still survives as it has Grade II listed status and the Ordnance Survey is obliged to continue to maintain the exterior.

Millbrook School, in nearby Green Lane, was built by Hampshire County Council in 1938, superseding an 1825 school in Wimpson Lane. The new building opened with 367 pupils on 27 April and catered for all age groups. By then many of the surrounding fields had been developed, with new roads such as Kennedy and Lancaster Roads in the vicinity. However, many of the pupils had farm addresses, showing that much of the immediate area was still very rural. This is reflected in the fact that unlike most Southampton schools, the children were not evacuated during the war years. Most of the Maybush area was in the county until the 1954 boundary extension, when the school transferred to Southampton.

In 1955, following the construction of Mansel Road Infants School, it became a secondary mixed school. New premises were built in 1960, divided into separate boys' and girls' schools, but the two schools amalgamated again in 1967 to become Millbrook School, a neighbourhood co-educational comprehensive school. It is now known as Millbrook Community School with pupils transferring there from the neighbouring Primary and Junior Schools.

A distinctive and rare feature of this school today is its 'Down To Earth' school farm. This dates from the 1930s and 1940s, when gardening was on the curriculum, with many pupils still country children who helped their parents on

The Ordnance Survey Office original building in London Road. The buildings had been erected in 1800 as cavalry barracks and in 1816 they were converted to a military asylum (orphanage) for boys, serving as a branch of the Royal Military Asylum at Chelsea. The boys were removed to Chelsea in 1823 and replaced by orphaned girls. Some of the buildings were destroyed in the 1940 Blitz. *(Norman Gardiner Collection – Bitterne Local History Society)*

their farms. This school farm continued into the 1960s and the boys were given allotments to run, with foodstuffs grown from seed for sale. Pigs, poultry, chickens and bees were kept, with the produce sent to market and the profits ploughed back in. It is now a Local Education Authority resource, run by a manager qualified in rural studies and visited by children from Infant and Junior schools from the surrounding area. It still has a range of animals, with sheep, ducks, goats and a cow added to the former stock.

The school is overshadowed by its neighbouring massive Ordnance Survey complex. This organisation, initially known as the Trigonometrical Survey, was founded in 1791 with the initial task of mapping areas of Kent, Sussex and Surrey as a precaution against a Napoleonic invasion. The first non-military OS maps were produced from surveys begun in 1805, at a scale of one inch to one mile. This was to prove a most popular scale that would evolve through innumerable editions for more than two centuries.

The survey work continued after the end of the war with France in 1815, with the intention of mapping the entire country. This time three different scales were used, one inch, six inches and 25 inches to the mile. The six-inch scale was introduced in 1825, when a survey of Ireland was carried out for taxation purposes. The very large-scale maps often show the exact shape of even the smallest of buildings.

The Ordnance Survey was then based in the Tower of London but a severe fire in October 1841, when the Small Armoury was destroyed, badly damaged their quarters. Alternative offices were quickly found in London Road, Southampton, and staff moved in on the afternoon of 31 December that year. This was to be the Ordnance Survey headquarters for the next 101 years.

In 1938 there was a parliamentary recommendation for the introduction of a metric National Grid as a reference system for all maps. It also

The ultra-modern Ordnance Survey Headquarters, facing the main Romsey Road near Maybush Corner, *c.*1995. It was built on the site of the former Crabwood House Estate, which had been partially occupied by the Ordnance Survey since the war damage in London Road in 1940. *(Southern Daily Echo)*

the mile maps produced in 1947, carrying the OS National Grid references. This grid provided the first truly national map referencing system, whereby every place has its own unique location reference number.

By 1951 the number of Ordnance Survey staff peaked at 4,800, spread throughout the country. Technical changes in map making and surveying techniques, together with a system of small survey offices set up across the country, known as 'Continuous Revision' sections, soon reduced their numbers. However, new scientific and technological changes meant that the old buildings were no longer suitable for the efficient production of modern maps, and on 1 May 1969 HM the Queen officially opened a new purpose-built headquarters at Maybush.

All branches of the OS office were centralised in the modern headquarters, which saw the development of the new digital technology that transformed the well-developed map-making skills of the staff. The introduction of a digital database of map information, use of orbiting satellites and electronic theodolites are but a few examples of the rapidly advancing technology that has been continuously developed at Maybush. Large-scale maps can now be stored on a computer database and coded so that a customer buying them can clearly distinguish buildings, road networks and water features, all in colour.

Although the organisation is currently considering relocation, the impressive Ordnance Survey buildings and 22-acre site still dominate the Maybush area, having brought the cutting edge of modern technology into what was only recently a quiet rural backwater on the outskirts of Southampton. Much of the area's rural charm, however, remains.

included changes from a county to national basis for the 1:2500 (25 inches to the mile) maps, larger 1:1250 (50 inches to the mile) scale for densely populated areas and a trial of a 1:25,000 (two and a half inches to the mile) medium scale map. Before these recommendations could be implemented heavy air raids on the nights of 30 November and 1 December 1940 resulted in several direct hits on the Ordnance Survey Headquarters. Ironically, the German bombers were using OS maps that they had overprinted with their targets!

Much irreplaceable material was lost and some of the buildings were completely destroyed. However, the essential wartime production of military maps continued unabated, with the buildings temporarily repaired and the headquarters moved to Chessington. Staff were then working in different and scattered offices, some of them very basic, but the war effort was uninterrupted.

The end of the war saw the earlier recommendations implemented, with the first 50 inches to

Further Reading

Ordnance Survey Office *Ordnance Survey – 1791–1991*, O.S.O., 1991.
Wilkinson, Rosaleen *Millbrook, The Hidden Past*, R. Wilkinson, 2002.

Merry Oak

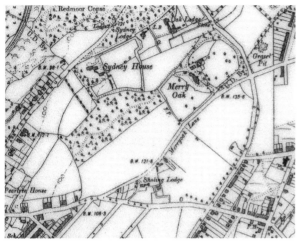

Merry Oak was still very much in the country in 1911, but Merry Oak House, owned by George Errington, was beginning to show signs of neglect. Merry Oak Lane (now Road) had yet to become the estate's southern boundary and the gravel pit to its east, bordering Spring Road, was one of many in the district. *(Reproduced from the 1911 Ordnance Survey map. NC/03/17894)*

THE origin of this name is obscure but alternative theories have been put forward. Phillip Brannon's 1887 guide book mentions the hamlet of Merry Oak, in the small dell near Pear Tree Green, and states 'The people of this locality in years bygone used to meet for dancing and merry-making round an ancient oak that now, in desolation, lifts its scathed leafless, blasted and shivering branches high.' His map shows this oak to be in the vicinity of the junction of Sholing and Wodehouse Roads, and it may well have been a boundary landmark to be celebrated with merry-making. However, it has also been suggested that the name comes from the Anglo-Saxon 'maer-ea-ac' – the oak of the boundary stream. There is, in fact, an underground stream in this vicinity, so either alternative is a possibility.

It is known that a house called Merry Oak was built about 1800 and that the Ede family purchased the house and estate in 1810. They also owned a nearby house called Oak Lodge. The estate had a number of owners, the last being George Errington who bought it in the early 1870s. When he left in 1920 the house, which had fallen into disrepair, was demolished.

Merry Oak Road was then a tree-lined Merry

A heavily wooded Spring Road at the junction with Blackthorn Road, *c*.1900, showing the area's rural aspect. *(Bitterne Local History Society)*

Looking north along Merry Oak Lane (now Road), at its junction with Sholing Lane (also now Road), *c.*1900. This is now the southwest corner of the Veracity Ground. The building is not to be confused with Sholing Lodge, which was a few hundred yards further north. *(Bitterne Local History Society)*

Oak Lane in pleasant rural surroundings. The expansion of Southampton in 1920 meant that Merry Oak, along with neighbouring Bitterne, Peartree, Sholing and Woolston, was absorbed into the borough, but it continued to be very much a rural area. However, Southampton Corporation purchased its attractive 51 acres for £32,567 by Compulsory Acquisition in 1928, as part of a national initiative to provide affordable housing for all. The town planners wanted to break away from featureless Victorian terraces and therefore made a number of demands on the developers.

As many trees as possible had to remain, with a minimum stipulated number, and any of those lost had to be replaced. No long straight roads

The junction of Merryoak Road, Spring Road and Deacon Road, *c.*1931. The Merry Oak public house, built about this time for Brickwood's Brewery, stands on the corner of Deacon Road. Note the now-vanished telephone kiosk on the left, outside today's Sonic TV, and what would now be a vintage car on the right, behind the signpost. *(Bitterne Local History Society)*

Mrs Florence Bedford outside 92 Magnolia Road, Merry Oak, at the Coronation of George VI in May 1937. *(Bill Monk)*

could be built, making the estate safer for children. There had to be a mix of housing and each had to have a bathroom and inside plumbing. This was a modern feature that broke away from the old concept of a privy in the backyard and a zinc bath hanging on the wall that was brought indoors for the weekly bath!

Main doors were either at the front or side of the house and all had fenced gardens at the front and back. A number of houses had external timber framing with exposed ceiling beams – others had bay windows and were called 'Parlour Houses'.

By June 1929 a total of 334 of the planned 616 houses had been built and Oak Lodge was laid out as a Corporation depot. Good landscaping was incorporated, with some parkland areas attractively fenced. The main drive to the former Merry Oak House, with its mature trees, was developed as Cypress Avenue and the majority of roads were named after ornamental trees or shrubs.

With the anticipated influx of children a school also had to be provided, but the slump of 1931 meant the first section was not opened until

Looking along Spring Road towards Peartree Avenue, *c.*1945. The view has not altered much, but the shopkeepers at this period, from left to right, were: A.E. Manning, Tobacconist & Confectioner; the Post Office run by Eric Baynton; D. & L. Meddick, Greengrocer; Donovan Battrick, Hairdresser and the Laurel Stores, run by Mrs E. Abbott. *(Bitterne Local History Society)*

1935. It catered for 120 boys and 111 girls aged between 11 and 12 years. However, pressure on school places was so great that a new wing, facing Acacia Road, was built the following year to accommodate a further 138 boys and 143 girls.

The outbreak of World War Two meant that, in common with other local schools, Merry Oak School closed temporarily on 1 September 1939 and many of the children were evacuated to Poole and

Merry Oak Road 'Parlour Houses', with fenced gardens and bay windows, in 2004. Built in 1929, they had the then modern feature of an inside bathroom and plumbing!

Parkstone. The school soon reopened for those pupils who had chosen not to be evacuated and they were joined by the similarly remaining girls of Sholing Girls' School.

The school was badly damaged in November 1940 when two classrooms sustained a direct hit overnight by a bomb, and again in June 1942 when incendiary bombs destroyed four classrooms, but teaching continued unabated. In July 1945 all the girls left Merry Oak and resumed their education in the new girls' school that had been built just before the war but not yet taken into use. Merry Oak School then became a Secondary Boys' School with 316 on its roll.

Falling numbers and educational reorganisation resulted in the closure of the school to new entrants in 1984, the existing pupils continuing in

the annexe as students of Bitterne Park School until the building's final closure in 1986. It was later demolished and replaced by housing, apart from a section that became a Community Hall. This has become a focal point for those residents who retain the spirit of the area, as shown by a 'Merry Oak Reunion' organised by the Tenants' Association and held in the hall in September 2000. Present and former residents then met to reminisce and view the local books on the area (listed below) and memorabilia from the school salvaged by Bitterne Local History Society.

Although the number of original residents is naturally dwindling, Merry Oak retains much of its original identity and character and the area continues to display the model placed upon its developers in 1928.

Further Reading

Croxson, E. *The Story of Merry Oak School*, Bitterne Local History Society, 2000.
Rolfe, J. *Memories of Merry Oak Estate*, Bitterne Local History Society, 2001.
Ward, R.V. *Memories of Merry Oak,* Sholing Press, 1987.

Millbrook

including Freemantle, Regents Park and Wimpson

THE 1086 Domesday Book records Millbrook, in Mansbridge Hundred, as follows:

> The bishop himself holds Melebroc. It always belonged to the monastery. In the time of King Edward, as now, it was assessed at 5 hides [600 acres]. Villans [villagers] held it and hold it. There is no hall. There is land for 5 ploughs. [A plough is the estimate of the arable capacity of an estate in terms of the number of eight-ox plough-teams needed to work it.] There are 28 villans with 5 ploughs and 14 acres of meadow. There is woodland for 5 pigs. In the time of King Edward and afterwards, as now, worth 100s.

In Old English the name implies a mill stream, and this fits in with a mill known to have been driven by a tributary of the nearby River Test.

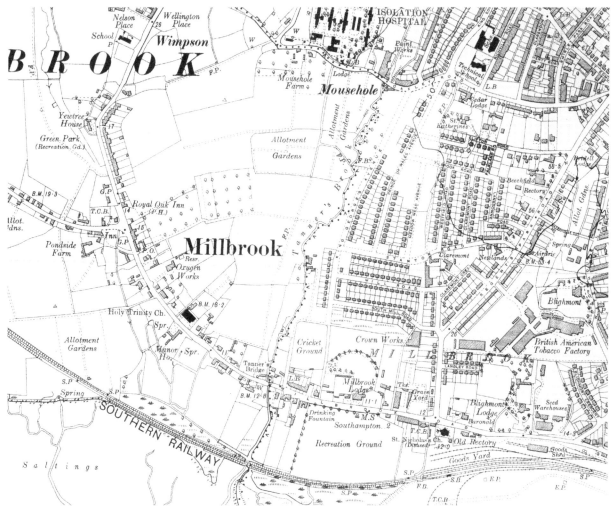

By 1931 the Isolation Hospital (also known as the Chest Hospital) and the British American Tobacco Factory were firmly established. Some may consider them to be opposing forces! Blighmont can be seen just north of the BAT factory. *(Reproduced from the 1931 Ordnance Survey map. NC/03/17894)*

Western Shore, Millbrook, c. 1920. Behind the fence is
Millbrook Railway Station, opened in 1861 but closed in
1967. The area was redeveloped as a Freightliner Terminal in
1968 and the shoreline vanished when the ground was
reclaimed for the construction of the Western Docks in 1932.
(Norman Gardiner Collection – Bitterne Local History Society)

Blighmont Crescent, Millbrook Road, *c.*1922, when it first
appeared in the street directories. A leading figure in the early
1800s, Admiral Sir Richard Bligh, built Blighmont, an eight-
bedroom mansion in an estate of 50 acres to the west of
Waterhouse Lane, for his son, Captain George Bligh. George
had been badly wounded on HMS *Victory* at the battle of
Trafalgar while serving as Lord Nelson's flag lieutenant. The
family were distantly related to the Captain Bligh of the notori-
ous 'Mutiny on the *Bounty*'. *(Norman Gardiner Collection –
Bitterne Local History Society)*

The Manor of Millbrook covered a large area,
over 3,000 acres, and included Shirley and
Redbridge, but the modern Millbrook is now
only the former southern portion. John Mill, a
wealthy merchant who was also in charge of vict-
ualling the armed forces, became Lord of the
Manor in 1545 and the Mill family continued to
dominate the area up to and including the 20th
century.

The name of the Freemantle district, in the east
of Millbrook, is thought to originate from the
French 'Fromentel', meaning 'cold cloak' and the

name of a forest. It may be that this area was
heavily wooded and exposed to the wind coming
from the nearby seashore, but the reason for the
name is otherwise unclear.

During the Great Plague of 1665 all normal
trade ceased in Southampton, but a market was
set up at Four Posts, in the west of the town, so
that residents of the country areas of Hill, Shirley
and Millbrook could supply food to the townspeople. They transacted their business by hoisting
goods over the stream at Rolles Brook, near
Achard's Bridge, with the money placed in a basket that was dropped into the stream to prevent
infection. Four Posts was given its name from the
four directional signs erected at the junction to
show the way to Millbrook and Redbridge to the
west; Romsey and Shirley Hill to the north-west;
Hill to the north-east and Southampton to the
east.

Southampton's spa period in the mid-18th century brought changes to the hitherto agricultural
Millbrook village as the fashionable gentry
sought estates and fine houses on the outskirts of
the town. One such was James Amyatt, who purchased Freemantle Park, an estate of over 140
acres, in around 1775, and transformed the existing house into a fine Georgian mansion. He had
made his fortune as a merchant with the East
India Company and was Southampton's Member
of Parliament from 1784 to 1807. The house

George Ayles stands proudly outside his grocery shop and post
office at 22 Testwood Road, at the junction with Marchwood
Road. However, he is only shown here in the local directories
of 1921 and 1922, so his tenure was short lived. *(Bill Moore)*

Park Road, Freemantle, *c*.1915. On the left is William Permain's grocery shop, next door to that of Sidney Foy, the linen draper. On the corner of Mansion Road is the Swan Inn, dating back to the early 1860s, known as the Wellington Arms since 1975. *(Bill Moore)*

boasted something that was extremely rare in the 18th century – a heated greenhouse!

General Sir George Hewitt bought the estate in 1822 and his family continued to own it until 1852. The family coat of arms can still be seen on the outside of the Shirley Hotel. The estate was then bought by Samuel Payne, a builder, who immediately demolished the house and divided up the land for development. Further 'genteel' properties were built in the Regents Park area in the early Victorian period and western Millbrook became a much sought-after district for those who wanted easy access to the town but wished to live in an elegant and refined district.

The poor were not neglected by the gentry and a Poor House and Parochial School, opened in 1819 near the site of the modern Bricklayers' Arms in Wimpson Lane, was well supported by private charities. Unfortunately for the residents' families the Poor Law Act of 1834 meant that parishes merged, with the result that in 1837 the inmates of the Poor House were rehoused in the South Stoneham Poor House at West End and the house and grounds sold. A new schoolroom had been built in the grounds of the Poor House in 1825 and this remained in use until 1938.

The 10th baronet and Lord of the Manor, Sir

Charles Mill, had left his estate to his nephew, John Barker, who was created baronet in 1836 and took the name Barker-Mill. An extravagant person, by 1852 Sir John Barker-Mill suffered financial problems and was forced to lease land in Millbrook for building to accommodate Southampton's increasing population. He died in 1884 and the estate was left to a distant cousin, Marianne Vaudrey, who added Barker-Mill to her name.

When both Shirley and Freemantle were incorporated into Southampton Borough a few years later, in 1895, housing quickly developed along the eastern boundary and the Millbrook parish was reduced to 986 acres.

It was Marianne Vaudrey Barker-Mill who stopped the building in Millbrook of what would have been one of the largest Ford Motor Company works in the country. The company had purchased 21 acres of mudlands at Millbrook Marsh to construct a deep-water quay for the import and export of cars and components, but hadn't appreciated that the Barker-Mills owned the foreshore rights. In 1922, when plans were well under way, she demanded a rental of £200 per acre, something that Henry Ford refused to pay. Neither side would give way,

Millbrook Towers, overlooking the homes around the Windermere Avenue district, c.1995. This 25-storey block, designed by Ryder & Yates of Newcastle-upon-Tyne, was officially opened in May 1965. (*Southern Daily Echo*)

with the end result that Dagenham's gain was Southampton's loss! (That is, until 1958, when Ford acquired a site at Swaythling).

Ford sold the area to the Southampton Corporation, which built a sewer works and a small three wooden military hut 'Millbrook Marsh' isolation hospital on the site in 1929. The hospital replaced the 'fever ship', the *City of Adelaide,* which had been anchored off Millbrook Point since 1893, catering for the isolation of smallpox and dangerous infections brought into the town by sailors returning from abroad. This was in addition to the purpose-built Isolation Hospital built in Oakley Road in 1898, with the Millbrook Marsh wooden huts still used for many years for the dwindling number of smallpox cases. Millbrook foreshore, of course, was reclaimed in the 1930s and is now part of the Dock complex.

The fine house Blighmont became a nursing home in 1921, until 1963 when it was demolished to become part of the British American Tobacco site. This company had purchased 18 acres of land at Blighmont Park in 1925 but it had not included Blighmont House and its gardens. BAT, as it is commonly known, remains firmly established in Millbrook to the present day and its large factory complex remains a constant source of valuable local employment. The site was enlarged with a further five acres in 1967 when BAT took over the grounds of the adjacent long-established firm of Toogood's Seed Merchants. This company, established in 1815, had been on the Millbrook Road site since at least 1920 and held a Royal Appointment as 'The King's Seedsman'.

In 1954 Southampton once again extended its borough boundaries, this time taking in the remaining unabsorbed part of Millbrook. This resulted in the major Corporation housing development of Millbrook council estate, designed in the garden-city tradition with the construction of 3,217 dwellings, including a number of tower blocks. Some 500 acres were purchased from the Barker-Mill estate and the first phase started between Wimpson Lane and Oakley Road. A new main road was opened in 1953 and given the name Tebourba Way in honour of the Hampshire Regiment's North African battle honour in December 1942.

An ever-expanding industrial estate was established to the south of this main London road and today the former agricultural land of Millbrook, with Freemantle, has a population of around 27,500 and is firmly established as a major part of the City.

Further Reading

Wilkinson, Rosaleen *Millbrook, The Hidden Past*, R. Wilkinson, 2002.

Northam

including Chapel, Kingsland and St Mary's

This plaque over an entrance in Brinton's Road states 'This site was once part of the Anglo-Saxon town of Hamwic. From about AD 700 Hamwic was a royal town, administration centre of Hampshire and an important trading and manufacturing centre in northern Europe. Goods from France, Belgium, Holland, the Rhineland and Scandinavia came into Hamwic. Its community of craftsmen in many trades, merchant and seafarers, was Christian, with a church where St Mary's now stands. From about AD 850 trade suffered from the effects of warfare in northern Europe and the Viking raids, and by AD 900 Hamwic was virtually abandoned.'

THIS is thought to mean 'north hemmed in land' in Old English and this fits well as the area is hemmed in by the final great bend of the River Itchen before it arrives at Southampton Water. It can also mean 'northern homestead', according to the *Dictionary of British Place Names* and this also fits well.

Northam was the first significant seventh-century Saxon town in the area, known as Hamwih or Hamwic. 'Ham' is the element that refers to an area hemmed in, in this case by the rivers Test and Itchen surrounding the peninsula. 'Wih' means a fortified centre and 'wic' means (among other things) the riverside trading settlement that surrounded it. Its street grid pattern still survives today in many of its modern roads, such as Chapel Road, Derby Road, Marine Parade, St Mary's Road and St Mary Street.

Hamwic was probably one of the largest densely populated towns in eighth-century England and possibly the only place in the country that ranked with the great trading centres of the Continent. Its ancient wooden Saxon minster, believed to have been founded in AD 634, is perpetuated today in the impressive 19th-century mother church of Southampton, St Mary's. This is the source of the well-known song *The Bells of St Mary's*, made famous by the late Bing Crosby. It was firebombed in the Blitz of 1943, with only the outside walls left standing, but re-roofed and re-consecrated in 1956.

The remains of a crucible, used to melt gold, have been discovered by archaeologists at a development in St Mary's Street, together with a black stone with tiny flecks of gold on one side. This would have been used as a touchstone to test the purity of precious metal. It suggests that Hamwic had at least one gold jewellery maker, making pieces for royalty and possibly for trading with Denmark or France. On the other hand, jewellery on three skeletons excavated from under the Friends Provident St Mary's stadium is believed

Golden Grove sign, erected in 1999. The children of St Mary's School designed the monumental panels with local artist Edmund Sayer. The large panel is based on the stylised animal and bird shapes found on silver coins minted in Hamwic about 1,200 years ago.

Cross House, 2001. Recently restored, this ancient structure has four sections to provide shelter no matter what the direction of the wind. It stands at the ancient landing place for the Itchen Ferrymen on the town side of the river. A tradition, recorded in 1719 but unsubstantiated, says it was erected through the bequest of an old lady who 'caught her death of cold' while waiting for the ferryboat. It is probably of mediaeval origin as there is a record of it being rebuilt in 1634.

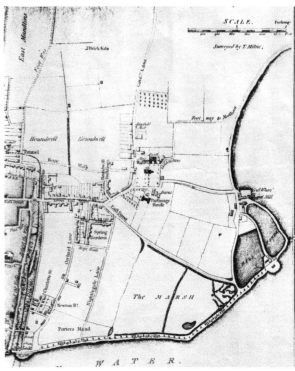

This plan of the town, made by T. Milne in 1791, clearly shows the large area of marshland in the south that was developed for working-class housing when the docks were constructed in 1840. Love Lane, running north to south, became St Mary Street and St Mary's Road and the agricultural fields that had served the town were transformed into cheap terraced housing and polluting industrial premises.

to have originated in Europe. One piece of jewellery had an animal chasing its tail and another showed a crescent moon. This suggests that Hamwic had established strong trading links in such commodities. It was almost certainly a large town with a well-organised community engaged in overseas trade and small-scale industrial production.

Archaeologists were surprised by the richness and quality of the materials found during the excavations for the stadium, which is in the oldest part of Hamwic. It was a prestigious Saxon graveyard, almost certainly noble or royal, and a remarkable sword found there was one of only two found in the country. The site was formerly home to the Southampton Gas Company, who now sub-let it to the football club. A little known fact is that the actual landlord is St Mary's Church, who leased it to the Gas Company many years ago for 999 years at an annual rental of 12 shillings and sixpence (62½p) with no review! The rent paid by the club to the Gas Company is not known, but it will not be measured in pence. The church ownership is possibly a throwback to the area being its ancient burial ground.

A valuable commodity for the inhabitants was salt gained from the area around today's Saltmarsh Lane, where the land curved to form an open lagoon that dried out at low tide. (A deed of 1704 also mentions several areas of pasture, including an estimated 45 acres of 'Milstone Marshes', whose name probably comes from an

This section of a 1911 map vividly demonstrates the growth of the area following the mid-19th century expansion of the nearby docks. The riverside is now crammed with wharves and the density of the housing is very apparent. Only the mediaeval parks, the city's pride and joy, remain to remind us of its former open spaces. *(Reproduced from the 1911 Ordnance Survey map. NC/03/17894)*

ancient tide mill on the west bank of the river Itchen.) The town's importance can be gleaned from the large number of silver 'sceatta' coins that have been found, believed to have been minted in the town. Its royal control and centre of local administration makes it almost certain that Hamwic was the site of the royal mint of King Beorhtric (AD 786–802). It is no coincidence that the small Northam districts of Kingsland and Queensland are so named.

The town was exposed to attack on its eastern shoreline and suffered from Viking raids, to the extent that by the 10th century the inhabitants had settled in the west of the peninsula. Here they felt more protected by the high ground adjoining the River Test. Hamwic was abandoned and allowed to fall into decay. Much of it became marshland and the remainder was taken into use for agriculture and livestock, hence the Threefield Lane and Hoglands Park of today. It lay outside the walled town of mediaeval Hamtun, although

A rare view of the interior of the Auguste Pellerin Margarine Factory in Princess Street, Northam, *c.*1899. An Act of Parliament that year permitted the manufacture and sale of margarine and this factory was the first of its kind in the country. Fat from the abattoirs of Paris was delivered three times a week, in barrels sealed with plaster-of-paris, and turned into a product called Le Danske. Sundew margarine and Laughing Cow processed cheese were also later made here. The latter can still be obtained although it is now produced in France, where margarine was first produced. Margarine came about when Napoleon offered a prize for the best substitute for butter, which was won by a Mr Mege Mouries.

In March 1837 James Wheeler, a local baker, constructed Southampton's very first purpose-built Primitive Methodist Chapel in St Mary's Street. He conveyed the property to the Trustees in 1840 for £400 and it was later enlarged and improved at a further cost of £520. The site was aptly chosen, in the heart of the working-class Kingsland district, an area that was rapidly expanding because of the massive dock expansion taking place nearby. It became the Oddfellows Hall in 1887, until 1966 when it was sold to a turf accountant. The basement, originally the Sunday School, became a club showing 'adult' films in 1975, compounding the drastic changes of use that would have horrified its original owners.

A now vanished Six Dials, c.1905, so called because it was the junction of six roads: Northam Road, St Mary Street, New Road, St Andrew's Road, St Mary's Road and St Mark's Road. The No.36 tramcar has just travelled down St Mary's Road from Stag Gates and is crossing the Dials to go down St Mary Street. St Mark's Road is on the right, on the corner of which, at No.137 St Mary's Road, is the general shop of James Rock. *(Henry Brain Collection – Maureen Webber)*

the ancient mother church of St Mary's continued to be important, with access via the town's East Gate in what we now know as East Street.

The district known as Chapel is aligned with Northam and lies to its south, with church-owned land in between. Its name originates in the Trinity Chapel built near the old mill and an annual Trinity Fair survived in Chapel for several hundred years. Both Chapel and the old Northam were used for shipbuilding during the 17th century and this continued well into the 19th century.

An important change came when Northam Bridge was built in 1799, opening up a new eastern trade route out of the town. New Road soon

The happy occasion in St Mary Street is probably Queen Victoria's Diamond Jubilee in 1897. On the left, adjoining the Kingsland Tavern, which dates to the early 1820s, is the edge of the now almost defunct 'Kingsland Square Market'. The stalls of the local traders were well frequented and were very much part of the local scenery. On the right of the unpaved street, on the corner of Bevois Street, is the large tailor and outfitter's shop of Baker & Co., while on the opposite corner, proudly displaying Union flags, is Percy Horder's Toy Repository. *(Henry Brain Collection – Maureen Webber)*

The South Western Hotel, *c.*1910. Adjoining the Southampton Terminus Station, the town's first railway station, opened in 1840, this five-storey building began as the Imperial Hotel, on the corner of Canute Road and Terminus Terrace, in the 1860s. It was taken over from its bankrupt developer by the London & South West Railway Company and renamed the South Western Hotel in 1871. At the top right, almost hidden by the trees, can just be seen the mast that supported a 'time-ball', operated electrically from Greenwich from 1904 to 1933. This dropped at exactly 10am daily so that mariners could check their ship's chronometer. Following many enlargements over the years the block has recently been refurbished and turned into luxury apartments. *(Bill Moore)*

linked the expanding town with the bridge and this encouraged the industrial development of the area. By 1804 the old Chapel shipbuilding yard had been turned into one of the first cargo wharves that would transform the banks of the river. Chapel and Northam were still villages at this period, with a scattering of houses amid fields and market gardens and employment in the increasing number of wharves along the river.

A dramatic change, however, from rural to urban life came about after the foundation stone

Northam Railway Station, *c.*1910, looking towards the Mount Pleasant crossing. Opened by the London & South Western Railway in 1872, adjacent to the old Northam Road Bridge, this station served the local inhabitants well for many years. The bridge was rebuilt with its present large girder framework surround in 1908. It fell into disuse, with the platforms removed and buildings demolished, in 1969, but there are current demands for it to be reopened to serve the nearby Friends Provident St Mary's Football Stadium. *(Bill Moore)*

was laid for the new Docks in 1838. The docks needed labour for both their construction and their operation and this labour needed cheap and basic housing. This soon appeared in Chapel, mainly conforming to the old field system, and from the first terraces in Millbank Street similar housing rapidly spread throughout the area.

There was a population explosion. St Mary's parish increased from 4,708 inhabitants in 1821 to 14,885 by 1841. The population there was said to be 'chiefly of the lower orders'. By this time much of Northam along the shoreline was also used for industries that provided local employment. Among these were linseed mills, artificial manure works, soap and candle works, lime and cement works and a brickyard, none of them ideal neighbours for the residents!

The author has fond memories of visiting his grandparents in their rented terraced house in Wharf Street, Chapel, in the late 1930s. Grandfather was a coalporter and his home was typical of the period. The front door, never locked, led direct from the narrow pavement into the sole living room packed with Victoriana and wall-mounted large family photographs. From here one entered the tiny scullery that led directly into a very small back yard, with brightly whitewashed walls on which hung a large galvanised

The premises of D.H. Beak, Baker & Pastrycook, 129 St Mary's Street, standing on the corner of Bevois Street, *c.*1927. It had previously been used by Percy Horden as a Toy Repository. The initial mere provision of teas flourished and by the 1950s it had become 'Jock's Restaurant', also catering for weddings and dances. Next-door is the pawnbroker, Charles Hooper, very necessary for the local population and an essential fact of life. 'Best suits', only worn at weddings and funerals, were pawned, with the added benefit of being held in good condition until redeemed for the occasion. *(Bill White)*

bathtub that was taken into the scullery on bath nights. The outside privy improved my childhood reading as the toilet paper consisted of torn squares of newspaper impaled on a nail on the inside of the door! A narrow staircase led from the living room to two very small bedrooms with a communicating door. It beggars belief that grandmother reared the survivors of her 11 children in such primitive, but spotlessly clean, accommodation. One thing is certain, there was an extremely strong community spirit, borne out of their shared poverty and uncertain work prospects, dock labour being casual and dependent on the varying needs of the shipowners.

Several schools had been built for the children of Northam and Chapel by the end of the 19th

A 2004 view of the Northam/Chapel area, with the spire of St Mary's Church rising in the centre, taken from the new Itchen Bridge. The former Saxon town of Hamwic and subsequent densely populated 19th-century working-class housing have been replaced by light industry and warehousing. The modern Friends Provident St Mary's Football Stadium on the right covers the Saxon royal burial ground that preceded the Victorian gas works.

century, the most impressive being the Eastern District Board School at the junction of Anglesea Terrace and Albert Road. It had an imposing rooftop playground with a surrounding safety rail and commanded a fine view across the busy docks.

14 April 1912 was a black day for the downtown residents. The sinking of the *Titanic* caused a massive crowd to besiege the White Star offices in Canute Road for information about their loved ones. Sadly, of the 900 crew 699 were from Southampton and the overwhelming majority of these were from the Chapel and Northam areas.

World War Two was an even blacker period for the district, which suffered massive damage because of its close proximity to the docks. Large areas were devastated and post-war development, coupled with the construction of the Itchen Bridge in 1976, completed the destruction of the close-knit community. However, work is currently being carried out on a £22 million scheme to turn part of the Chapel area into an urban village, incorporating 152 flats and 22 family homes. This part of the city is coming to life again, evoking memories of its bustling Saxon heritage.

Erected in December 2002 at a cost of £65,000, the 'Northam Shoal' stands almost 40ft high in Old Northam Road. Illuminated by fibre-optic cables at night, it consists of more than 800 stainless steel fish and depicts a group of individuals working together to form a community, as well as the tide of football supporters who flow through Northam to the nearby Friends Provident St Mary's Football Stadium. Old Northam Road is the home of internationally known antique shops, in particular 'Cobwebs', whose owners specialise in shipping artefacts and memorabilia, especially those connected with the *Titanic*.

Further Reading

Gale, J. *Children of Northam 1900–1930*, Davis Printers, 1990.

Hodgson, Maie *Child of the Ditches*, Fleetwood Print, 1992.

Jemima, Sheila *Chapel & Northam*, Southampton City Council, 1991.

Pay, Sharon, *Hamwic, Southampton's Saxon Town*, Southampton City Museums, 1987.

Pelham, R.A. *The Old Mills of Southampton*, Southampton City Council, 1963.

Rance, A. *Shipbuilding in Victorian Southampton*, Southampton University Industrial Archaeology Group, 1981.

Southampton Archaeological Research Committee, *Saxon Southampton*, 1975.

Peartree

including Itchen Ferry Village

The Pear Tree, planted December 1951 by the Mayor of Southampton, Councillor Mrs M. Cutler OBE, is protected by a secure iron fence. Tradition has it that Queen Elizabeth I planted the first tree but there is no evidence to support this. In 1803, when there was a threat of a French invasion, the Duke of Cumberland staged a mock attack from the River Itchen near this spot.

THE origin of the name Peartree is perpetuated by a solitary pear tree on Peartree Green, a wide expanse of high open grassland, with fine views down the river and across to Southampton. It was a remote rural area, much of it undeveloped heathlands, used by the fishermen and ferrymen of nearby Itchen Ferry Village on the banks of the River Itchen. They had the ancient right to ferry passengers across the river, granted by successive Lords of the Manors of Woolston and Southampton, the former being paid in cash and the latter in free passage for the Burgesses and their families. They also transported farm pro-duce from the surrounding area to help feed the Southampton townspeople.

Distinguished individuals were not averse to using the ferrymen's services. Diarist Samuel Pepys travelled across the Itchen by ferry in 1662, having ridden from Portsmouth, and dined with Southampton's Mayor, William Stanley, eating the roe of sturgeon. In 1669 Charles II was rowed across to Itchen Ferry Village when he visited the town.

The ferrymen guarded their rights jealously and were a breed set apart. They were also tough deep-sea sailors and weather-beaten fishermen who formed a close-knit community. They did not take kindly to strangers who might settle and encroach on their livelihood or be one of the despised excise men probing smuggling activities.

Itchen Ferry was also said to be the meeting

Peartree House, 2003. Built in the early 17th century, the crenellated stucco front of the building is thought to be the work of George Waring, a curate of Peartree Chapel, in the early 19th century. Its most famous resident was General Henry Shrapnel, inventor of the exploding shell, who lived there from 1835 until his death in 1842. Much of the land around the house was developed in the 1930s and in 1949 it was acquired by Southampton Corporation as an old people's home. It closed as such in late 1995, due to Health Authority reorganisation, and is currently a Rehabilitation Unit for Acquired Brain Injuries.

Peartree Church in 2003. Jesus Chapel, to give it its correct name, faces Peartree Green and was the first church to be built in England after the Reformation. It could originally seat 290 but when the North Aisle was built in 1847 this doubled its capacity. Inside are many memorials and tablets to the local gentry and although its churchyard has been closed for burials since the beginning of the 20th century many old tombstones remain standing to commemorate local families.

Peartree Athletic Juniors football team, 1909-10. *(Bitterne Local History Society)*

place of the conspirators against Henry V as he prepared to sail for the Battle of Agincourt in 1415. They were later executed in the town and the tradition is that their trial took place in the existing High Street public house, the Red Lion.

In the late 16th century Francis Mylles, later MP for Winchester, applied to the Bishop of Winchester for permission to cart some Roman stone from Bitterne Manor to build a new house. This was granted and Peartree House came into existence on part of Ridgeway Heath. It was occupied in around 1617 by one of Mylles's relatives, Captain Richard Smith.

Captain Smith, a former Governor of Calshot Castle, was said to be a pious and God-fearing man. He was concerned that although Peartree was in the Parish of St Mary's, it was on the opposite side of the river, often necessitating a rough crossing in an open boat. The only other available churches were in South Stoneham, Botley or Hound, involving either a very long walk or an uncomfortable ride over rough unmade roads.

He therefore decided to build, at his own expense, a church to serve the eastern area, the first church to be built after the Reformation. Jesus Chapel, also known as Pear Tree Church, was completed in 1618 and dedicated in September 1620, just after the Pilgrim Fathers left Southampton on their epic voyage. It is believed that more stone from Bitterne Manor was again used. This is very likely as the stone in the west wall is known to have come from quarries in the Isle of Wight that were exhausted several hundred years before the church was built.

The delay between completion and dedication was probably due to the negotiations over the payments due to St Mary's Church, then suffering severe financial problems. All marriage and burial fees had to go to the Rector of St Mary's,

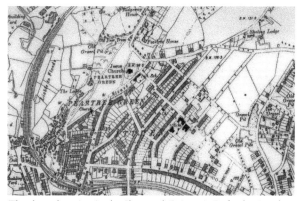

The dense housing in the Shamrock/Britannia/Defender Roads area of 1911, together with the scattered housing of Itchen Ferry Village north of Elm Road, were all swept away in the 1940 Blitz. The area east of the railway line is marked as being liable to flood, a worrying potential problem for the LSW Railway Company. Note the number of gravel pits. *(Reproduced from the 1911 Ordnance Survey map. NC/03/17894)*

Royal Oak, Hazel Road, c.1925. The original Royal Oak was on or near this site for several centuries, providing hospitality for those crossing the River Itchen by boat or Floating Bridge. Rebuilt for Cooper's Brewery at the end of the 19th century, it was demolished in the same air-raid that destroyed the nearby Supermarine Works in 1940. *(R.J. Parker & Son Ltd)*

regardless of the actual building in which they took place, and the upkeep of the new Chapel had to be borne by its parishioners, who also contributed towards St Mary's.

One feature of Jesus Chapel is the memorial stone to 17-year-old Richard Parker that states he 'died at sea on July 25th 1884, after nineteen days dreadful suffering in an open boat in the tropics, having been wrecked in the yacht Mignonette'. A gruesome story and sensational murder trial lies behind this brief inscription.

The *Mignonette*, with a crew of four, had left Millstone Point, directly opposite Pear Tree Green, on 19 May 1884, en route to Australia. One of them, young Itchen Ferry orphan Richard Parker, was making his first voyage. The vessel foundered in heavy seas on 5 July, and the crew were left adrift in a 13ft dinghy. By the 20th day afloat, with no food or drink, the boy was delirious and dying, having drunk seawater. A decision was then made by the others to sacrifice him to save themselves. His throat was cut and the blood divided between them, and they lived on his body for the next four days until rescued.

At their eventual trial for murder at Exeter Assizes their defence was that the circumstances justified their act of cannibalism. The matter was taken before the High Court, and two of the accused were convicted and sentenced to death. However, this was commuted to six months imprisonment, such was the sympathy for their predicament. The case ranks high in case law on the interpretation of justifiable homicide.

By the second half of the 18th century, with the expansion of Southampton as an important spa, the gentry thought it highly desirable and fashionable to live on the eastern shore of the Itchen, with its fine views across Southampton Water and vast areas of undeveloped land. This had the initial effect of increasing the trade and income of the ferrymen, but as the population expansion on the east side increased, demands grew for better communication across the Itchen.

The consequent building of the Northam toll

The General Shop and Post Office, *c.1925*, on the corner of Fletcher's Cottages. The name on the sign over the shop is Bower, the successor to the Smith family. The Yacht Tavern to its right in Hill Street (later Sea Road), built in the 1850s, was originally owned by Fuller, Smith and Turner's Brewery, but is now a Courage house. It was rebuilt at a cost of £8,700 and re-opened in January 1957. *(R.J. Parker & Son Ltd)*

The right-hand house in this Itchen Ferry Village scene was owned by the Smith family and built *c.1820*. The small house next to it is said to have been built around an upturned boat, the outline of which can just be seen to the extreme right of the picture. *(R.J. Parker & Son Ltd)*

bridge in 1799 had some effect on the ferrymen's trade, but their eventual demise came with the creation of the Itchen Bridge Company in 1833. After abortive alternative schemes and several false starts, the eventual success of their new Floating Bridge at Woolston finally spelt the end of a lucrative trade for the Itchen ferrymen. Their only compensation was the right to use the Floating Bridge without toll and for their wives and children to only pay half toll. They continued with a night rowing boat service for several decades, until the Floating Bridges finally fully replaced them and the fiercely independent ferrymen of Itchen Ferry Village then became a relic of

a once proud past. They continued to find fame, however, as outstanding yachtsmen, crewing for rich gentry, such as Sir Thomas Lipton, in early 20th-century races in the Solent.

In 1807 the Above Bar Congregation Church in the town started a 'Village Reading Society' to visit the villages around Southampton that the 'welfare of the villagers' might be looked after so they 'heard the Gospel'. The first station was opened at Itchen Ferry, where Mrs Skeates's home was used as a licenced 'preaching house'. A new building in Hazel Road, just off Oakwood Road, was rented the following year for regular services and a Sunday School started there in 1812. The Home Mission Society, formed in 1836, purchased the land in 1839 on which the present-day Pear Tree Green United Reformed Church stands. It opened in September 1840, with its members drawn from the old Itchen Ferry Village. In view of the subsequent small attendance and low income, it became the responsibility of the Above Bar Church in 1849, and this still applies.

The expansion of Southampton in 1920 meant that Peartree, along with its neighbouring Bitterne, Sholing, Woolston and Weston, was absorbed into the borough, resulting in closer ties and improved communications with the town. The proprietors of the Northam Bridge denied Southampton Corporation the use of the bridge for their bus service; so retired Warrant Officer

The shoreside and entrance of the Woolston Supermarine Aviation Works in 1928. It was their chief designer, the inspired genius Reginald Joseph Mitchell, who created the planes that won the coveted Schneider Trophy outright in 1931. It is, of course, for the renowned Spitfire that he is best remembered. Sadly, he died in 1937 before he was able to witness their triumph during the Battle of Britain. *(Norman Gardiner Collection – Bitterne Local History Society)*

The upper stretch of Hill Street, now Sea Road. The Red Lion public house at 29 Sea Road, on the left, dates back to the 1830s. It was taken over in 1896 by Cooper's Brewery and destroyed in the bombing of 1940. The railway bridge at the bottom of the road was constructed by the LSW railway for the line that opened in March 1866. It was to the right of this bridge that an air-raid shelter received a direct hit, with many fatalities, when the nearby Supermarine building was attacked. *(R.J. Parker & Son Ltd)*

Douglas Easson immediately invested his army gratuity in a coach and started the first bus service for the area. It ran from the Woolston side of the Floating Bridge to Butts Road, later extended to Hedge End Village, and their garage was alongside the Chamberlayne Arms in North East Road. The service was augmented, and eventually replaced, after the Corporation bought Northam Bridge in May 1929 and used a fleet of six large six-wheeled buses to serve the eastern side of the River Itchen. This local family business, with its fleet of modern coaches, continues to provide a service to the community with national and international holiday tours.

The close-knit Itchen Ferry Village disappeared in the bombing of World War Two, due to its close proximity to the Supermarine Aviation Works. This had started in October 1913 as a factory to produce marine aircraft with a ready-made runway on the doorstep. Its founders were Noel Pemberton-Billing, an eccentric inventor,

and Hubert Scott-Paine, a motorboat enthusiast. It was their intention to 'build boats that fly rather than aeroplanes that float'.

This ambition was fully satisfied after 22-year old Reginald Joseph Mitchell, from Stoke on Trent, joined them in 1917. During the next 20

Wharncliffe Road in Itchen Ferry Village, c.1941, following the destruction of the area when the nearby Supermarine factory was attacked. The area was used for Commando training in house-to-house fighting prior to the D-Day landings. Post-war planning resulted in the former village being transformed into multi-storey flats and light industry. No trace now remains of the former shops or public houses, other than the rebuilt Yacht Tavern. *(Joan Holt)*

years, until his death from cancer in 1937, he designed many sea and land based commercial and military flying boats, creating World Air Speed Records and winning the highly acclaimed Schneider Trophy outright for Great Britain in 1931. It was his genius, of course, that brought the famous Spitfire fighter into being, the clinching factor in winning the Battle of Britain.

It was the great success of this aircraft, manufactured on the Itchen waterfront, that spelt disaster for both the factory and the Peartree district. Sustained enemy air attacks in September 1940 not only demolished the factory but also virtually destroyed the whole village, with over 100 individuals killed.

The area was used as a training ground in house-to-house fighting for Commandos prior to the D-Day landings and further developments during the construction of the Itchen Bridge in 1976 removed almost all remaining evidence of the original buildings. They have been replaced by a number of light waterside industries and modern housing developments under the shadow of the massive Itchen Bridge.

Although the modern political Peartree Ward, that includes most of Itchen, currently has a population of around 14,500, only a fraction of that number are housed in the original Itchen Ferry Village area. However, the well-known family names of Adams, Cantel, Chapman, Cooper, Cozens, Dagwell, Diaper, Jerram, Jurd, Leburn, Parker, Thompson and Tucker, although now spread throughout the world, maintain their emotional attachment to the now vanished village.

Further Reading

Barfield, Norman *Supermarine*, Chalford, 1996.

Brown, Jim *The Sad Tale of Richard Parker*, 1997.

—— *Bridging the Itchen*, Bitterne Local History Society, 2002.

Cleverley, Audrey *Focus on Woolston*, Sholing Press, 1981.

Corps, D.E. *The Story of Jesus Chapel*, Pear Tree Church, 1985.

King, R.G. *Itchen Ferry Village*, 1981.

Galbraith, Ann *The Diaper Family of Itchen and Woolston*, Bitterne Local History Society, 2003.

Local Studies Group, *Woolston & Sholing*, 1984.

Mitchell, Gordon *Schooldays to Spitfire*, Tempus Publishing, 2002.

Mornington, Gerald *Southampton's Marquis and other Mariners*, Dorset Publishing Co., 1984.

A 21st-century view of what used to be the old Itchen Ferry Village. The slipway in the centre foreground was used to launch flying boats from the Supermarine Works, destroyed in September 1940. Industrial premises have replaced the ferrymen's homes and the train in the centre right is en route to Portsmouth via Woolston Station, travelling on the railway line that bisected the village in 1866.

Polygon

including Banister Park and Fitzhugh

THIS district owes its unusual name to a development that started in August 1768 as a self-contained block of properties designed as a regular dodecagon. Southampton was then at the height of its spa period, fostered by Frederick, Prince of Wales, when he made a visit in 1750 and found its seawaters 'salubrious and invigorating.' Although he died a few months later his sons, the Royal Dukes of York, Cumberland and Gloucester, continued to visit the town and attract the aristocracy.

The town rapidly expanded as a watering place; new elegant houses were erected and bathing establishments and assembly rooms flourished, a favourite being the Long Room on the West Quay. However, this meant passing,

A 1783 engraving of the Polygon complex, the cornerstone of which bore the date 9 August 1768. A letter written in August 1771 stated '...every house has a most beautiful view of the sea and the town of Southampton. There is a most magnificent hotel, in which there is a fine ballroom, card, tea and two billiard-rooms, several eating rooms and they say fifty good bed-chambers and stabling for 500 horses. There are to be all sorts of elegant shops in this hotel; at present there is only a jeweller and a hairdresser. I never saw so great a preparation both for luxury and elegance.'

either on foot or in sedan chairs, along dark, dirty and undrained side streets that were too narrow for carriages. Persons 'engaged in trade' also frequented the Long Room and those who believed themselves to be superior decided they needed a more select centre for their amusements.

The grandiose project was therefore started on a 22-acre site, north-west of the town. It was to be within an encircling carriageway and consist of 12 large houses with long gardens tapering behind them, like the spokes of a wheel, to a central basin of water. It also included 'a capital building with two detached wings and colonnades, of which the centre was an elegant tavern with assembly rooms and card rooms', the whole to be a venue for sparkling social occasions. Evidence of its status was shown by the foundation stone, laid on 9 August 1768, bearing the names of the town's two Members of Parliament, Lord Viscount Palmerston and Hans Stanley.

An 1802 view of the area, clearly showing the open public spaces of the West Marlands, used for public gatherings, leisure and travelling circuses. The Polygon development is only partially completed but the fine driveway is available for the gentry to drive round in their carriages. The section of the West Marlands to the left of the centre Redbridge/Romsey Road became the site of the town's Civic Centre, and the section on the right is now Watts Park.

Polygon Hotel, *c.*1960, rebuilt in 1937–8 on the site of the 18th-century Polygon House. The cornerstone, now displayed on the large block of flats that has since replaced it, was laid on 22 September 1937 by the Chairman of Polygon Hotel Investment Co. Ltd, Dr H.J. Bower. The architect was Jas E. Adamson, DSO, of London, and the local contractors were A.E. Jukes and Son. *(Bill Moore)*

This large block of 60 flats has replaced the former Polygon Hotel and displays a cornerstone placed on 2 June 2002 by the Rt. Hon. John Denham, MP. The flats were constructed by Barratt Homes and the architect was the Morgan Carn Partnership. It also has a plaque explaining that the 14th Major Port, US Army, was quartered here during World War Two, when they were responsible for planning and directing the movement of the US Expeditionary Force through the Port.

The tavern was constructed by 1771 and staged weekly 'Dressed balls' to attract a higher class of individual than the other assemblies at the Long Room and Dolphin Hotel. Indeed, the autumn Polygon assemblies were hosted under the patronage of two of the three Royal Dukes, the Duke of York having died shortly after the project started.

Unfortunately the ambitious scheme was afflicted with financial problems from its very beginning and it was never completed. One of the two main promoters was declared bankrupt in 1773 and they subsequently abandoned the project after having occupied two of the three houses that were built.

The Duke of Cumberland then rented one of the properties but this was not sufficient to continue to attract the aristocracy and it went somewhat 'downmarket' in order to remain viable. The central tavern was demolished soon after 1774 and replaced by houses, with several more also built on the line of the dodecagon. However, they were occupied by 'respectable families', as opposed to 'the nobility and gentry', and the envisaged grand project never materialised, although the circular gravelled road remained for some time.

The district slowly developed in the mid-1800s with the construction of several fine houses with pleasant balconies and railings, and by the end of the century one of the original large houses became a hotel again, called the Polygon.

The area was transformed after 1905, when John William Newcombe of Market Harborough and his partners in the Newcombe Estates Co. bought some 23 acres of land in the Polygon and adjacent Terrace House estate. This estate was centred on the site of the Baptist Church, built in 1910 and sponsored by John Newcombe, at the junction of Kenilworth and Devonshire Roads. The entire area was then fully developed into the street pattern so familiar today.

A relatively unknown feature of this area is the outstanding stone portrait gallery that can be seen on the fronts of five pairs of semi-detached houses, numbers 4 to 22 Kenilworth Road. They are of 10 famous literary men and are well worth a visit.

Directly opposite the earlier Polygon project was the former East & West Marlands, a name derived from the word Magdalens, after the mediaeval leper hospital that used to be there. They became the cultivable plots of common fields that only became available for common

Nos 4 to 22 Kenilworth Road, the Polygon. Charles Meadows, a local mason, made 10 pairs of beautifully carved heads, in Bath stone, on the fronts of these houses. They are mounted below the bedroom windowsills and each has a fine floral decorated surround. Full details of the subjects and the craftsman who made them can be found on page 22 of A.G.K. Leonard's *More Stories of Southampton Streets.*

pasture after the crops had been harvested at the time of Lammas. In the 19th century the Lammas rights were bought by the corporation and the fields turned into common parks, a position that continues to the present day.

The north side of the West Marlands became known as Watts Park after the statue of one of Southampton's famous sons, the hymn writer Isaac Watts (1674–1748) was erected there in 1861. Watts Park also houses the prototype of Whitehall's Cenotaph, designed by Sir Edwin Lutyens and inscribed with the 2,008 names of Southampton's World War One dead.

The southern side of the West Marlands is home to the City's prominent Civic Centre, the result of the personal commitment and dedication of Alderman (later Sir) Sidney Kimber. Its foundation stone was laid by Prince Albert, Duke of

The inauguration of the new road in front of the Civic Centre on 6 July 1932 by the Duke and Duchess of York. A small portion of the Thorner's Charity Homes can be seen on the right. *(Bitterne Local History Society)*

The Civic Centre in 1938, soon after its construction. The 156ft-high clock tower strikes the chimes of Isaac Watts's *O God Our Help in Ages Past* every four hours, from 8am to 8pm. The imposing front entrance leads to various civic offices, as well as the Council Chamber, via impressive twin stone staircases. The left-hand side houses the Police Station and the Law Courts, with their own entrance on the west, grouped around a very fine barrel-vaulted public entrance hall. The beautiful Rose Garden in the front, with its 22 beds of roses, was swept away in post-war road developments and the fountain moved to the north of the building, in front of an Art Gallery that houses exceptional art collections. *(Peter Heard)*

The Cenotaph, inside the entrance to Watts Park. Designed by Sir Edwin Lutyens, RA, this World War One memorial was built at a cost of over £9,000 and unveiled in November 1920. It has the words chosen by Rudyard Kipling 'Their Names Liveth for Evermore' cut on its west face and is inscribed with the 2,008 names of those Sotonians who fell in World War One.

York, (later King George VI) in 1930 and it was fully completed by 1937.

The Polygon district is today home to a large number of Southampton University students, many of the original properties having been converted into bed-sits, and the older residents are beginning to understand the meaning of 'town and gown'.

Further Reading

Kimber, Sir Sidney *Thirty-Eight Years of Public Life in Southampton*, Privately Published, 1949.
Leonard, Alan G.K. *More Stories of Southampton Streets*, Paul Cave Publications, 1989.

Portswood

including Portswood Park and Westwood Park

No 324 Portswood Road, a Grade II listed building and lodge to the first Portswood House. built in 1778 by General Giles Stibbert of the East India Company. It has been a blacksmiths, a car sales office and is currently empty and for sale. In 1968 the then owner tried to obtain a demolition order, but strong local resistance triumphed and the application failed.

OLD maps show that the Manor of Portswood originally included the modern Bevois Town, Swaythling, St Denys and Highfield, but these are now suburbs in their own right. The name comes from the Old English 'Porteswuda', meaning 'wood of the town' and there is evidence from the Roman occupation of Clausentum that a lot of timber was needed for smelting iron in the adjacent St Denys. A document of 1254 also mentions that '...the canons of St Denys have and hold a certain wood called Portswood by a grant from Richard, formerly King of England, in free, full and perpetual aims.' This was granted in 1189. Portswood then had 'three plough-lands, three groves of woodland, 100 acres of pasture, 40 acres of meadow and 40 of marsh.' Its labourers had to work hard for the Priory, just as they had done for the King. They had to clear half an acre of ground each day, from John the Baptist's Day (24 June) to 1 August, and in August they had to reap half an acre each day, for which each man received a sheaf. When the harvest was over they had to collect clay for repairing their houses,

The horse drawn tram at Portswood Junction, c.1900, has just left the depot and is passing the Belmont Inn at No.200 Portswood Road. This building was demolished in the 1920s and the Belmont Hotel built on the site. *(Henry Brain Collection – Maureen Webber)*

The same view in 2004. The Belmont Hotel was renamed the Mitre in July 1986 and became a free house in 1994.

The Brook Inn, No.466 Portswood Road, at the junction with Belgrave Road, c.1900. The pair of horses are carrying a full load of passengers on the horse bus. The public house dates back to the 1860s. (Henry Brain Collection – Maureen Webber)

Tennyson Road c.1900, built by Henry Brain, builder, with members of his family standing in the front porchways. They would occupy the buildings until such time as tenants were obtained. The fine railings protecting the small front gardens were all removed as part of the war effort during World War Two. (Henry Brain Collection – Maureen Webber)

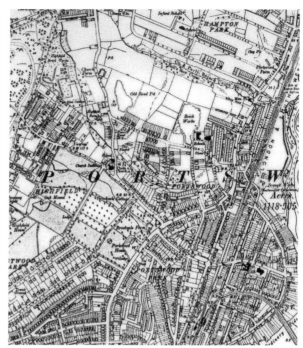

Dense housing had developed in lower Portswood by 1910, although Portswood House and its lodge continued as a private estate, adjoining Brookvale Farm. The Hampton Park area, however, was still mainly open fields and sandpits. (Reproduced from the 1910 Ordnance Survey map. NC/03/17894)

gather apples to make cider, shear sheep, carry out repairs and make up the fences.

The Prior, as Lord of Portswood, agreed in 1396 that its inhabitants should 'submit to the jurisdiction of the town' and in 1469 there is the first mention of the 'Alderman of Portswood'. He represented Portswood at the town's Court Leet and was, in effect, their constable.

In 1524, during the reign of Henry VII, it was Southampton's poorest ward, and only 21 persons in the tithing had assessable goods for taxation. Eighteen of these were in the lowest category of only £1, compared with all the other wards that had householders in the higher grades of £10 and more. The Prior's ownership continued until Henry VIII dissolved the Priory in 1538, when Sir Francis Dawtrey purchased both the

Manor and the St Denys district. Portswood was then very thinly populated and by 1696 only had 73 inhabitants.

Jointly with St Denys, it had a succession of owners, including the Earl of Peterborough in 1730, and became very desirable during the town's rise as a spa. It was during this period that Walter Taylor, renowned for his invention of the circular saw and specialist block-making for the Royal Navy, built Portswood Lodge. This was a fine mansion with extensive grounds and stood on the west of Portswood Road, almost opposite the junction with St Denys Road. The estate extended to 200 yards back from the main road and ran from Highfield Lane to Brookvale Road. Its 32 acres of pasture were used in 1844 for a huge Royal Agricultural Society Cattle Show that catered for several thousand visitors.

General Giles Stibbert, of the East India Company, later purchased the Portswood estate. He built the first Portswood House around 1778

Joseph Harvey's shop at No.35 Portswood Road in 1911. He was a Gilder and Picture Frame Maker with further premises in St Mary's Street and the Strand in town. *(Norman Gardiner Collection – Bitterne Local History Society)*

Portswood, thus provided fine country retreats for the fashionable gentry, but the eventual decline of the spa, and consequent reduced prosperity for the borough, brought change. People of high social standing found the area less desirable and were inclined to dispose of their properties and move further afield. The growing power of steam and proposals for new docks also meant that the sparsely populated outer districts were ripe for development, to cater for Southampton's increasing need for housing.

It was against this background that a developer acquired Portswood House in 1834 and built houses in the grounds. The building was demolished in 1852 for further housing and the sole surviving remnant is the Grade II listed building of 324 Portswood Road, its former entrance lodge.

on a site now bounded by Spring Crescent and Lawn Road and it was said to have given 'fine views across the entire Itchen Valley.'

The immediate outskirts of the town, such as

The Palladium Cinema, Portswood Road, *c.*1953. Opened in 1913, this well patronised cinema could seat up to 650. Television affected its business and the last picture to be shown was *Murder at St Trinian's* in 1958. The adjacent Public Library was built in 1915 for £3,175, after the land had been purchased by Sidney Kimber (later knighted) and transferred to the corporation for the same price. *(Norman Gardiner Collection – Bitterne Local History Society)*

The same view in 2004. The familiar glass canopy along the length of the Palladium vanished when it became a supermarket.

Another building, Portswood Lodge, then became the second Portswood House when it took on that name by 1861. A new developer, Walter Perkins, bought it in 1875 and enlarged the estate in 1888 in the knowledge that it would gain in value. The area then consisted in the main of a scattering of prosperous merchant's villas and estates, and St Denys was becoming a new district in its own right. The break up and sale for building purposes of such large estates helped the process of filling up open spaces with streets of suburban houses and changing the character of the area.

The horse-drawn tramways connecting Portswood to the town had opened in 1879 and this also encouraged Walter Perkins to develop his holding. This was helped by the central horse tram depot opening in Portswood Road, near the bottom of Highfield Lane, with over 100 horses stationed there. This has continued as the hub of Southampton's tram and subsequent bus system.

Portswood Temporary Board School (a large room!) opened in 1899 and it is recorded that many of the children were very poorly clothed and shod. A soup kitchen was opened at the school for the area's poor and although a bowl of soup only cost a penny, between 150 and 200 families were entitled to free soup because of their poverty. It closed after six years and was replaced by a purpose-built Infants School that opened with 166 children.

After Walter Perkins died in 1907 his family continued the development of his land on 'garden city' lines, with further building along Portswood Road and Abbott's Way. More shops appeared, from Brookvale Road to Highfield Lane, together with the Palladium Picture Theatre and a public library. World War One disrupted progress, but work soon resumed and Portswood House was demolished in 1923. All the estate plots were sold by 1928 and the area's development was completed on its present lines.

Portswood, with its population of around 12,000, continues to be an attractive shopping area on the outskirts of the town, with a variety of individual small shops and pleasant housing.

Further Reading

Leonard, Alan G.K. *Stories of Southampton Streets*, Paul Cave Publications, 1984.
Local Studies Group, Southampton *Portswood, Personal Reminiscences*, 1982.
Ticehurst, Brian and Meachen, Harry *Pictures of Portswood's Past*, Kingsfisher Railway Productions, 1989.

Redbridge

THE name of this suburb, in the extreme south-west corner of Southampton and part of the old Manor of Millbrook, comes from the Old English 'Hreodbryecg', meaning a bridge where reeds grow. This still applies, as the marshy area, adjoining the now derelict former bridge over the River Test, continues to show an abundant display of reeds.

This bridge, now derelict, was part of the main west road from Southampton and as such was of great strategic importance. In March 1644, when the Parliamentarians held Southampton, the Royalists advanced as far as Romsey and captured the bridge at this point, then made of wood. They were stopped from advancing further by a Parliamentarian force under the command of the Squire of Alresford. The bridge was partially destroyed in December 1643 when Lord Hopton, the Royalist general, retaliated after his Romsey forces were attacked by the Southampton garrison. *(Henry Brain Collection – Maureen Webber)*

An illustration on steel and wood by Robert Mudie of Redbridge in 1838. The Redbridge Village houses are on the left and soldiers with crested helmets have crossed the central causeway and are riding across the bridge towards Totton. They are following the tail end of a coach or cart laden with passengers. The sailing boat is moored downstream on the River Test. *(Norman Gardiner Collection – Bitterne Local History Society)*

The 1086 Domesday Book survey reveals a sparsely populated Redbridge:

> Hugh himself (Hugh de Port) holds 1 hide (120 acres) in Rodbrige. Tovi held it of the King. Then, as now, it was assessed at 1 hide. There are 4 villans (villagers) and 1 bordar (cottagers, peasants of lower economic status than villans) with 1 plough and 2 mills rendering 50s, and 1 acre of meadow. In the time of King Edward, and afterwards, it was worth 10s, now 60s.

The boundary between the mediaeval parishes of Eling and Millbrook (of which Redbridge was a part) was in the centre of the river, but it was the Redbridge residents who made a living from cutting the reeds on the eastern side. They obtained further employment when William Myatt, a Bursledon shipbuilder, built the 32-gun *Winchelsea* at Redbridge in 1694. More ships followed, especially when Samuel Bentham, the inspector-general of naval works, chose the area to design and build six experimental ships designed to save timber in their construction.

At this period a long causeway across the marshes from Totton, passing over a small side stream, gave access to a wooden bridge over the main channel. However, the causeway was subject to frequent flooding and the situation was greatly improved in 1793 when its height was raised, the side stream widened and a new stone bridge constructed over the river. This came about because of the area's increasing reliance on shipbuilding and the completion of a canal to Andover the following year. The canal was 22 miles long, with 24 locks, and was large enough to take barges 65 feet long by eight and a half feet wide. It was in use for the ensuing 60 years, car-

Tanners Brook, *c*.1920. The stream, now running under the road, was a source of power for several mediaeval mills along its length, probably mainly used to grind corn. Some of them had changed into foundries by the mid-19th century. Another local industry, tanning, i.e. turning animal skins into leather, was also almost certainly carried out, giving rise to its name. Cornelius Williamson, a Tanner of Millbrook, appeared in the 1656 records and Tanners were recorded in Millbrook up to the late 19th century. *(Bill Moore)*

rying such goods as slate, coal, manure and a variety of agricultural products.

A further canal was started, to connect Southampton with Salisbury, but it was beset by difficulties. Its new cutting, constructed along Millbrook shore as far as Redbridge, passed along the line of the modern Gover Road to join the Andover canal, but it experienced severe engineering problems. Abandoned in 1808, it fell into disuse and was eventually destroyed in the 1860s.

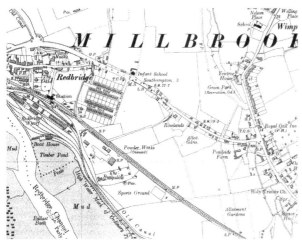

The small mansions of Clover Nooke, The Oaks and Roselands still survive in 1931, but Redbridge Wharf now has a concentration of busy railway sidings. Traces of the old disused canal are shown to the north of the area. *(Reproduced from the 1931 Ordnance Survey map. NC/03/17894)*

Redbridge's shipbuilding industry went into decline after 1843 but this loss was replaced three years later when the railway came to Redbridge, with a small station provided by the new Southampton & Dorchester railway. There was a double line to Southampton but only a single line to Dorchester via Ringwood, along a timber viaduct built over the River Test.

The situation was enhanced in 1880 when the London & South Western Railway purchased Redbridge Wharf and adjacent land, where they established a Permanent Way Works, access to which was controlled by a level crossing and signal box. The railway then became the main employer of the village and an important depot for track maintenance.

By 1884 the lines from Redbridge to Totton and Romsey had been doubled, the passenger accommodation on the station improved and the platforms lengthened. This vastly improved transport system encouraged local manufacturers and such industries as linseed oil production, vitriol works, creosoting plant and even a gunpowder company, to establish factories in the vicinity. All this provided much needed local employment, and with it came a need for increased housing. A

A 1945 photograph of wartime 'Dragons Teeth and Knife Rest' anti-invasion roadblock defences erected in 1940–41 in Millbrook Road near the Borough boundary with Redbridge. *(Southampton Archive Services)*

number of buildings were constructed for the railway workers and several of them still exist today.

Redbridge then began to experience the effects of Southampton's ever-increasing growth and need for expansion. The borough boundary was extended as far west as nearby Tanner's Brook in 1895, almost reaching Redbridge, and this temporarily satisfied Southampton's needs. A new parish council then administered the remaining area.

All Redbridge west/eastbound traffic had to make a sharp turn opposite the Anchor Inn, over a controlled railway crossing (known as 'Test Gate'), a narrow stone bridge and the Totton causeway. With the increased popularity of the motor car in the early 1920s this became a worsening bottleneck and remedial action became

A bogie wagon, fitted with small hand cranes to help with loading and unloading, at Redbridge Works in 1958. Note the neatly packed tall stacks of railway sleepers on the wagons in the background. *(Associated British Ports)*

essential. The solution was to build a new concrete bridge that spanned both the railway and the River Test at a higher level, and work started in 1926. It was eventually completed in 1930 by Hampshire County Council, helped by the Ministry of Transport and the Southern Railway Company, at a cost of £100,000, and opened by the foreman of the Redbridge Works, Robert Gillingham. The new bridge and approach road to the east made a spectacular improvement to the traffic situation, bringing peace to the bypassed Old Redbridge village.

Southampton's need for expansion came to the fore again in 1954, when its boundary was again extended, this time to include the whole of Millbrook, including Redbridge. Wholesale development soon followed; one effect on Redbridge being the construction of a new Millbrook roundabout, with a dual carriageway leading to a new roundabout at Redbridge. This main western approach to Southampton was to serve the proposed container port and Docks, eventually linking up with the M271 motorway at Redbridge.

Dramatic high-rise development came to the area in 1963 when the 20-storey Redbridge Towers block, home to 114 families, was opened. (The political Redbridge Ward now has a population of over 14,500.)

State-of-the-art technology arrived in 1996

Redbridge Towers overshadows the wide sweep of the flyover that leads west to Totton, *c.1995*. This crosses Redbridge Roundabout, built in 1964, which leads to the start of the M271, just out of sight behind the Towers. Both the Millbrook and Redbridge flyovers were completed in the late 1970s and provide direct access to the city centre. Old Redbridge village, with scattered blocks of modern flats in its eastern section, lies to the left of the flyover. *(Southern Daily Echo)*

when the *Southern Daily Echo* relocated there from its city centre site. Originally incorporated as the Hampshire Advertiser County Newspaper and Printing and Publishing Co. Ltd in 1864, it produced the town's first daily publication, the *Southern Echo*, in 1888. It continues to this day to be very much an independent local paper, focused on objective accurate reporting of local events and not subject to the extreme distortions found in much of today's national media. Its printing facilities at Redbridge are so modern that

they are also used for the production of other national newspapers.

Further revolutionary hi-tech equipment is also on the cards for Redbridge. A pioneering 'green' scheme to provide cheap heat to 4,000 homes in the area is currently planned. A gas-fired plant will be built on a piece of land at the city boundary, between the M271 slip road and Redbridge Lane, and the first homes supplied with instant hot water in 2005. This will bring the former sleepy bypassed old village firmly into the 21st century.

Further Reading

Totton & Eling Historical Society, *Redbridge Yesterdays,* 1996.
Wilkinson, Rosaleen *Millbrook, The Hidden Past*, R. Wilkinson, 2002.

Shirley
including Hill, Upper Shirley and The Common

Map of the Common in 1866. The 'New Reservoir' is in the north-east corner, on the site of the former town gallows. Further down, in the centre of the marked 'Old Racecourse', is Reservoir No.3, later called 'The Boating Lake'. Reservoir No.2, which eventually became the site of the paddling pool, is just above the Cowherds public house and north of Hawthorn Cottage. *(Reproduced from the 1866 Ordnance Survey map. NC/03/17894)*

The Cowherds Public House, the Common, in 1906. Built about 1762, this was originally the home of the town's cowherd. He cared for the livestock owned by the town's residents, who alone had the 'Rights of Common' to graze their animals there. One of the earlier cowherds also brewed beer, which he sold from his home. This prospered so well that by 1789 it had become the 'Southampton Arms', but as the locals insisted on calling it 'the cowherd's house' it reverted to its current title by the 1870s. *(Peter Heard)*

THERE are two versions of the Old English origin of this name. It is either a 'bright wood clearing' or a 'shire wood clearing'. A 'bright wood' is a sparse one, as distinct from a shady wood, and a 'shire clearing' refers to a place held in common by landowners in a shire or county. Although there is no evidence that a 'shiremoot' (a mediae-val meeting of the freemen of a shire) ever met here, there may possibly be a connection between nearby Portswood as the wood of the town and Shirley the wood of the shire.

The 1086 Domesday Book records Shirley, in the Mansbridge Hundred, as follows:

The same Ralph (Ralph de Mortimer) holds Sirelei. Cypping held it of King Edward. It was then, as now, assessed at one hide. There is land for eight ploughs. There are four villans and three bordars with two ploughs. There is a church and five slaves, and a mill rendering 30d, and 12 acres of meadow and woodland for six pigs. In Southampton, four messuages, rendering 40d. There is a fishery rendering 6s. In the time of King Edward and afterwards, as now, worth 100s.

The Manor of 'Sirelei' was acquired in 1228 by Nicholas (of Shyrle) and was very probably cen-

Southampton Common, *c*.1905. In 1844 the Common was officially designated, by Act of Parliament, 'an area for public recreation' and this principle has never changed. Until the middle of the 19th century there were many other public areas for fairs, such as the Marlands, but these gradually developed into commercial sites. By the beginning of the 20th century the Common was the prime area for regular fairgrounds, with their numerous stallholders, barrows, tea tents and amusements such as swings, coconut shies and boxing booths, spread across the main footpath leading from Hawthorn Cottage (now the Hawthorn Urban Wildlife Centre). *(Henry Brain Collection – Maureen Webber)*

tred on the mill powered by the Hollybrook and Tanners Brook streams, at the junction with the modern Redbridge Hill, Romsey Road and Winchester Road. Nicholas was immediately involved in a dispute with the Southampton burgesses because he claimed the Common was part of his Manor and he thus held the grazing rights. This was eventually settled by Nicholas receiving payment of 10 silver marks for relinquishing his claim on the Common, giving the townsfolk the rights of pasturage for all time.

One interesting feature of the Common is the tree-encircled mound a few yards east of the junction of The Avenue with Burgess Road, known by its ancient name of 'Cutthorn'. It was once on the extreme north of the town's boundary and was where the Anglo-Saxon Folk Mote, afterwards known as the Court Leet, used to meet. This was the oldest law court connected with the town and enquired into crimes, the town's defences, trade regulations and the like. In more serious cases it made 'Presentments' to the Assizes or Quarter Sessions but dealt with lesser charges or complaints itself. This ancient tradition persists to this

Picnic on the Common, *c*.1905. The ladies are almost certainly governesses or nursemaids, taking their charges for a picnic in the mid-winter sunshine. However, the fine woman with the pram on the left is very likely the lady of the house, thus ensuring that a good quality tablecloth and serviceable china is in use. *(Henry Brain Collection – Maureen Webber)*

day, when complaints on various matters are brought to the attention of the City Council.

In 1272 Shirley Manor passed to the Barbeflete family, who had obtained their wealth by trading in wool and wine, and in 1290 they granted the use of the spring of Colewell at Hill (in lower Hill Lane) to the Franciscan Friars. Their Friary was at the lower end of Southampton High Street and by 1304 they had constructed a Waterhouse (preserved in Commercial Road) to collect the water from the spring and carry it in lead pipes to the town. Conduit houses were also erected outside All Saints' Church, Holy Rood and the Friary. The spring at Colewell was therefore the main source of water for the town, apart from the domestic wells in yards or gardens. Southampton was thus one of the earliest, if not the first, towns to have a piped water supply.

The area of Hill, at the eastern edge of the Manor and bordering the Common, appears to have been mainly agricultural land with a substantial farmhouse. However, there is evidence that artisans and craftsmen also worked there. Among them was a Robert Orchard at Hill, who in 1474 supplied the wood for a new Scold's Throne, for punishing 'those who would not please to moderate the rancour of their tongue'.

Edwardian ladies admiring the swans on the Boating Lake, Southampton Common, c.1907. Originally a man-made reservoir, created before 1846, the Model Yacht Club used this lake as early as 1894. It was then 15 feet deep in the centre with a terrace of four feet deep around the circumference. Following two deaths by drowning in 1919 it was filled with rubble to its present four-foot depth. (Norman Gardiner Collection – Bitterne Local History Society)

The Manor passed through various hands and late 15th-century records show that it was prosperous, with luxury goods such as French wine, figs, raisins and almonds delivered to the manor houses of Shirley. The Lords of the Manor from this period to the 18th century were the Whitehead family, after whom the modern Whithedwood Avenue is named and they remained very influential in town affairs and local government.

Southampton's decline during the late 17th century, due to the Great Plague of 1665 and a reduction in the wine and wool trades, must have had its effect on neighbouring Shirley, although few records are available. The Whitehead lineage came to an end with the marriage of the surviving daughter, Mary, in 1717 to Alexander Thistlethwayte, and the Manor was then progressively sold off, mainly to the Atherley family, who became the leading and most influential figures of the area. They were prosperous merchants, deeply involved in civic affairs, with many of them becoming Mayor, and by 1830 they owned practically all the land to the west of Hill Lane.

Southampton's spa period, from the mid-18th century, resulted in many fine estates and small select villas being developed in the Shirley district as the gentry sought the company of royalty and enjoyed the elegant balls and concerts in the town. The wars with France and Holland at the end of the century brought the army into the town and many of them were encamped on the Common while awaiting departure. One campsite is shown on an 1802 map as being near the top of Hill Lane.

The last public execution took place on the Common on 27 July 1785, when a former servant, Soane William Kerby Shayer, was hanged for entering his previous mistress's house in Above Bar and stealing her silver plate. It is recorded that he was placed in a cart covered with a black cloth and had a handkerchief placed over his face to 'avoid seeing the unusual con-

Shirley Church, *c.*1910, consecrated in 1836 by the Bishop of Winchester, on land given by Nathaniel Jefferys of Hollybrook House. St James' Church initially had seating for 600. Only four years later this had to be increased to 1,000 by the construction of balconies and further pews were added in 1881. These were all removed in 1994, when the floor was levelled and carpeted, with modern chairs replacing the old pews. *(Bill Moore)*

course of spectators who surrounded him.' The town gallows is now covered by the reservoir on the upper part of the Common, to the left of Winchester Road. There was also a racecourse south of the reservoir, dating from 1822, with a grandstand on the open plateau at the top, facing The Avenue. Its popularity varied considerably, with several declines and revivals, and the last race was held in 1881.

Shirley High Street Carnival, *c.*1895. Shirley was taken into the Borough this year, so the gentleman in the top hat in the open carriage with a mounted police escort is almost certainly the Mayor of Southampton. The London Central Meat Company premises show that the procession is in Shirley High Street and the flamboyant band of Cavaliers have just passed the junction with Pound Street (renamed Cannon Street in 1924, after Bitterne, with its Pound Street, was absorbed into the Borough). *(Henry Brain Collection – Maureen Webber)*

The growth of the ever-expanding Southampton in the early part of the 19th century resulted in the enclosure of Shirley Common in 1829. The following year plots were sold to individuals and roads were laid out, with 10 public carriageways, two bridleways and three footways. A number of large houses were built but the area was mainly occupied by market gardeners supplying the needs of the district. Many of the new inhabitants were wealthy merchants and shopkeepers from Southampton who abandoned their practice of living over their shops and moved to what was then considered to be the countryside.

An entry in the *Hampshire Advertiser* in 1836 encapsulates the changes:

> We are glad to observe the progress of the works, private and public, on Shirley Common. Villas are fast rising there, creating the appearance of a populous and genteel occupation of what is well known to be one of the most beautiful and healthy spots in our picturesque neighbourhood. The road is now complete

The Grammar School in Havelock Road, *c.*1904. King Edward VI School moved from its original 16th-century Winkle Street premises to nearby Bugle Street in 1696, where it remained until 1896. It then moved to Havelock Road, on the site now occupied by the BBC South studios, until 1937 when it became established on its present site in Hill Lane. Among its many famous ex-pupils are: Prof. Sir Edward Abraham; Isaac Watts, whose hymn *O God Our Help in Ages Past* is the school hymn; Rt Revd Michael Langrish, former Bishop of Exeter; Sir Ralph Metcalfe; George Gould, CBE, past president of the Royal College of Veterinary Surgeons; Dudley Kemp, former president of the Rugby Football Union; Sqdn Ldr John Merifield, DFC, holder of the high-speed record flight across the Atlantic; and Sir Sidney Kimber; the driving force behind the town's Civic Centre and Sports Centre. *(Bill Moore)*

Shirley High Street, *c*.1903. The White Hart Hotel is on the extreme right. Owned by the Winchester Brewery, it closed in 1982. Just beyond it, on the corner of Church Street, is the large boot and shoe store of William Gange and Sons. Tram No.40 has travelled to Shirley from Prospect Place on the town's first electrically operated route, which only opened three years earlier. *(Bill Moore)*

from Hill Lane through the Warriner's estate connecting the (Shirley) Common very readily with our town.

The old parish church at Millbrook, which

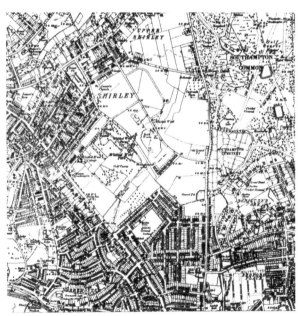

In 1907 the upper stretch of Hill Lane had the Common to the east and open fields to the west, with King Edward VI and the Girls' Grammar schools yet to be built. Housing has surrounded Hill Farm, in lower Hill Lane, and the area around the upper High Street, in the north-west, is also highly developed. Whithed Wood Park, to the east of lower High Street, contains a golf course. *(Reproduced from the 1907 Ordnance Survey map. NC/03/17894)*

served 2,375 parishioners in 1836, was clearly too small for the increased population to its north and the new St James' Church, on the corner of Upper Shirley Road (Bellemoor Road) and what became St James' Road, was consecrated that year. Within a few years its capacity had to be increased to accommodate a congregation of over 1,000.

Housing development continued throughout the century, although areas such as Bellemoor Road Nurseries and Hill Farm (Brown's Dairy) meant that much of it retained its rural character. Shirley was brought into the County Borough of Southampton in 1895 and this accelerated the development of the hitherto open areas. However, one small open space that persists to this day is the sunken and enclosed area of Shirley Recreation Ground. This was a worked-out gravel pit opposite St James' Church, owned by George Harris of Whithedwood Farm, and its six acres were purchased for £1,000 in 1907 by Southampton Corporation.

The eastern boundary of the district, Hill Lane, houses two important educational establishments – King Edward VI School and Taunton's College. The former is the oldest school in Southampton,

Shirley Road, *c*.1950. Emanuel, goldsmith, watchmaker and jeweller of 385 Shirley Road, heads the terrace of shops, next door to the well-known sports outfitters, Holt & Haskell. Arthur Holt was a Hampshire County cricketer and Reg Haskell was a former Mayor of Southampton. In the background is St Boniface's Roman Catholic Church, built in 1927 at a cost of £15,000, with its fine bell tower. *(Bill Moore)*

Taunton's College, formerly in Highfield, now occupies the Hill Lane buildings that previously housed the Southampton Grammar School for Girls. The Borough Council established this school in 1907 in new buildings in Argyle Road. In 1928, recognising their inadequacy, the council bought a 12-acre site off Hill Lane where it built a new school for 550 girls, completed in 1936 with generous provision for tennis and other sports. From 1967 the school developed as an open access Sixth Form College; in 1993 this was merged with Taunton's College, concentrated on the Hill Lane site, where the accommodation was further extended.

founded in 1553 with around 20 boys in Winkle Street, at the bottom of the High Street. Often referred to as just 'the Grammar School', it moved to its present location in 1937, but wartime evacuation in 1939 meant that the bulk of pupils went to Poole Grammar School for the duration of the war. It became an independent school in 1979 and by 1994 had become co-educational. It remains, with its rivals Itchen and Taunton's Colleges, one of Southampton's leading seats of learning.

Although Shirley's rural character has changed beyond recognition, it still remains a highly desirable residential area with a population of around 12,500, affording easy access to both the surrounding countryside and the City of Southampton. The well-maintained 375-acre Common to the east, with its four open lakes and pools, fine trees, the Hawthorns Urban Wildlife Centre and its open access, provides a wonderful readily available recreational area for the Shirley residents. Together with the beautifully maintained parks in the city centre, the Common acts as the City's lungs, to the benefit of all.

Further Reading

Guilmant, John *Shirley, A Series of Personal Reminiscences,* Local Studies Group, 1983.
Leonard, Alan G.K. *Shirley Nuisances & Services, Public Health & Local Government in Victorian Shirley,* Southampton City Council, 2003.
Local History Forum *Shirley, from Domesday to D-Day,* Southampton City Council, 1997.
Thompson, S.C. *Southampton Common,* City of Southampton Society, 1980.
Wilkinson, Rosaleen *Millbrook, The Hidden Past,* R. Wilkinson, 2002.
Velecky, Lubor *Protect It Now – A History of Southampton Commons & Parks Protection Society,* 2000.

Shirley Warren

including Aldermoor, Coxford, Lordshill and Lordswood

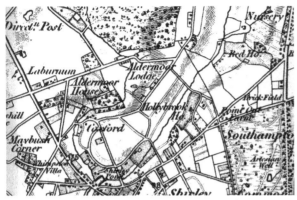

Map of the Shirley Warren area in 1864, showing that although there is a basic road network, there are few properties of any note. Aldermoor House and its lodge, with Hollybrook House, occupy the bulk of this predominantly rural area on the outskirts of Southampton. Hollybrook House, demolished in the 1950s, was built in 1836 for Nathaniel Jefferys and became a home for pauper boys in 1912. The upper part of the Common can be seen in the south-east corner. *(Reproduced from the 1864 Ordnance Survey map. NC/03/17894)*

THE story of Shirley Warren cannot be isolated from its immediate neighbouring sub-districts of Aldermoor, Lordswood, Lordshill and Coxford, and they are therefore included. All are within the ancient boundary of the Manor of Millbrook, as outlined in the Anglo-Saxon Charter of 956 and

were farmland within the county of Hampshire, until absorbed into Southampton by the 20th century.

Aldermoor takes its name from Aldermoor House and its lodge, built for the Barker-Mill family in 1800. It was once part of Nursling Common and the 60 acres of land remained in the Mill family until 1931, when it was sold to Southampton Corporation for building. Aldermoor House was surveyed and found to be unsuitable for conversion into flats. The Corporation Parks Dept. used its glasshouses for propagation in 1933 but its demolition took place shortly afterwards.

A further 13 acres, purchased in 1935 for £6,597, were to be used 'for educational purposes'. This gave rise to the construction of Aldermoor School, opened in September 1938 and extended the following year to accommodate 400 Juniors and 400 Infants. However, an additional four classrooms were provided for 'visiting children' – children from other Southampton schools who would visit regularly to use the class-

An aerial view of part of Aldermoor in 1995. Palm Road runs down from the top left, through the circular intersection with Alder Road. The triangular junction of Rownhams Road, Lancaster Road and Dolton Road is at the top right. *(Southern Daily Echo)*

Birch Close, Coxford, during a street party for the Coronation of George VI in 1937. This is good evidence of the very strong community spirit in this neighbourhood, with funds raised for the street decorations. Residents' household chairs were used, but a beer barrel and crate were needed for a bench seat! *(Dolly O'Beirne)*

rooms in the morning and the extensive playing fields in the afternoon.

The dangers of World War Two meant that the pupils were evacuated, half to Ringwood and half to Burley, in the New Forest, for its duration. American and Canadian soldiers, who were stationed there up to D-Day, used the school premises during the war. As a result of local education reorganisation in 1989 the school was demolished, with housing built on the site, and only part of its playing fields now remain. Pupils were absorbed into other schools already serving the area.

In spite of Southampton's expansion into Millbrook, Redbridge and Harefield in 1954, there was still insufficient land available for house building to satisfy its needs. Lordshill, with its 563 acres, was therefore purchased in 1964 to cater for this growing demand, with approval given by Hampshire planners for homes for 2,000 people to be built, and it was incorporated within the City boundary in 1967. The very old woodland of Lordswood, now developed, is just inside

the City boundary, to the immediate northwest of Lordshill, and adjoins the Sports Centre.

Lordshill was originally little more than fields and a dead-end road that dropped down from Old Rownhams Lane to Tanner's Brook, between the Bedwell Arms Public House and Aldermoor Road. This steep lane only had about six houses, with water frequently running down the road from various springs. It was known as 'soapsuds alley' because the washerwomen living there often threw their soapy water outside the front of their cottages, mixing with the spring water to create a foaming torrent.

Over 4,000 dwellings had been built there by 1982, about one-third by the private sector, and the lower density housing provided homes for about 12,500 people. A good range of facilities was also provided, including a large supermarket, a number of shops, a pub, library, church for the use of four denominations, several primary schools and a Community School (Oaklands). This school now has a Community Theatre that seats 200 in a raked auditorium and provides

Shirley Pond in 1906. It was then said to be the property of the Royal Mail Steam Packet Company who used the ice, cut from the pond in winter, on board their ships. The blocks were stored in old ice pits at the rear and this is reflected in the name of the Ice House Inn, 180 Warren Avenue, built near the site of the pits in 1912. (Bill White)

In 1900, when the Royal South Hants Hospital in the town was clearly failing to satisfy the needs of the growing population, the Poor Law Guardians purchased 35 acres in Shirley Warren for £8,200 to build a hospital. The foundation stone, laid on 6 March that year, is still preserved in front of the 1977 central block of the modern premises in Tremona Road. This photo was taken in 1901 with Henry Brain, one of the sub-contracted builders, proudly standing in front of his work. Called the 'Shirley Warren Poor Law Infirmary' (also styled the 'Incorporation Infirmary', harking back to the 1773 union of Southampton parishes for Poor Law and Workhouse purposes) the first phase cost £64,800 and provided 289 beds. It had its own kitchen gardens to provide fresh vegetables, its own herd of pigs, a substantial boiler room for its laundry and its own generating station. (Henry Brain Collection – Maureen Webber)

local and national small-scale theatrical and musical events. A further noteworthy development in 1982 was Manston Court, with its 60 self-contained flats that accommodate 122 senior citizens.

Coxford takes its name from a ford that crossed the dip in the lowest part of Coxford Road, with somebody by the name of Cox almost certainly living nearby. Southampton Council Minutes for 1936 give details of tenders for erecting 339 houses, 12 flats, 12 garages and 12 shops for a 'Coxford Housing Scheme'. A tender of £130,310 was accepted, together with a cost of £19,716 for providing roads and sewers. The construction was completed by June 1938.

Further post-war development took place, mainly designed by Herbert Collins's partner, J. Norman Calton. The site layout incorporated cul-de-sacs, grass-bordered winding roads and open-plan front gardens. Houses were built in a simple style, with rendered concrete walls and metal casement windows. Nos 32–34 Coxford Road display a plaque dated 1948 and those in nearby Thorndike Road and Hardwick Close were completed by 1950. Coxford Ward currently has a population of around 15,500.

Shirley Warren, an area of 35 acres, had been agricultural land for centuries, until purchased by Southampton Council for housing development

in 1920 at a cost of £6,600. Building did not start, however, until 1926 and by 1930 a total of 442 houses had been erected. The initial contract was for 72 houses along Warren Avenue, of the so-called 'Parlour Type', with two ground floor living rooms and three upper bedrooms. Some of them were built on the site of former brickworks that had been backfilled, so they were built on raft foundations. One particular area that was more difficult to build on was left as a recreation ground, and is retained as such to this day.

Shirley Warren's most dominant feature is the Southampton General Hospital. This has consistently expanded since its inception in 1900 as the Shirley Warren Poor Law Infirmary. It became the Borough Hospital in 1929, when Southampton Borough Council took over the responsibilities of the Poor Law Guardians and the number of beds increased to 431. The following year 336 surgical operations were performed and the average stay for all patients was 50 days. Its current name,

A sturdy traction engine pulling a large boiler at Shirley Warren, *c*.1900. It is thought that this is one of the boilers destined for the new laundry at the 'Shirley Warren Poor Law Infirmary'. *(Henry Brain Collection – Maureen Webber)*

Southampton General Hospital, followed the establishment of the National Health Service in 1948.

Among the modern improvements and additions are: the Wessex Neurological Unit in 1965; the new East Wing in 1974, providing a further 450 beds and a new Accident & Emergency Department and Children's Unit; the new Centre Block in 1977, built on seven levels and costing over £9 million; the separate Princess Anne Maternity Unit in 1980; the new West Wing with 472 beds in 1983, at a cost of £10 million and a Wessex Body Scanner, costing £1.5 million, in 1984. All this is in addition to the transfer of the Cardio-thoracic Unit from the Western Hospital and the transfer of Southampton Eye Hospital.

Southampton General is now a leading teaching hospital and part of Southampton University Hospitals NHS Trust. With around 900 beds, it is their flagship and has an international reputation for its outstanding research facilities. It is the main teaching centre for the Wessex region and provides highly specialised medical facilities, including cancer, neurological, cardiac, thoracic, ophthalmic and radiotherapy centres and paediatric surgery. Nearby, in Coxford Road, the over 200-bed Princess Anne Hospital specialises in obstetrics and gynaecology.

The Trust currently has more than 7,500 staff and its services cost in the region of £800,000 a day. In the course of a year the hospital deals with more than 350,000 outpatients, 115,000 in-patients and 85,000 emergency cases. There are current proposals for the construction of a new £53 million state-of-the-art cardiac centre, housed in a three-storey extension at the northern block of the hospital. This will help to deliver an extra 3,000 investigations and treatments a year.

To complement the medical services in this

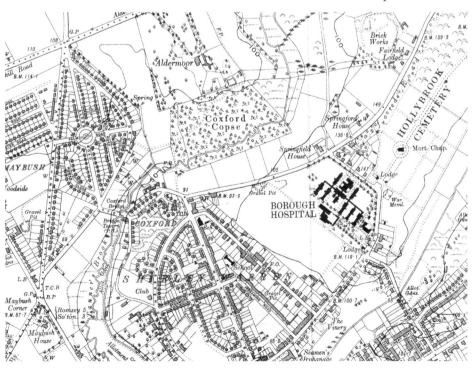

The Borough Hospital was well established by 1931, but the adjacent areas of Coxford Copse, Aldermoor and the unmarked Lordshill to their north, are still agricultural land. Extensive development has taken place in the Shirley Warren estate, centred on Warren Avenue, together with the small estate centred on Palm and Alder Roads to its north. *(Reproduced from the 1931 Ordnance Survey map. NC/03/17894)*

A 1995 view of the Shirley Warren Estate, looking south along Warren Avenue at its junction with Warren Crescent at the bottom of the picture. A portion of Laundry Road can be seen on the left and St Jude's Church is in the upper right. *(Southern Daily Echo)*

area, the private BUPA Chalybeate Hospital, with around 100 rooms, is practically adjacent to the Southampton General. It was opened in 1984 and provides a full medical service. It has also gained an international reputation for its heart, vascular and neurological services and offers a joint in-vitro fertilisation programme with the nearby Princess Anne Hospital.

Although the district's rustic character has long vanished, its value to the City, through its out-standing medical services, more than compen-sates for this loss. The original rural nature of the area has not been completely lost however, thanks to the network of 'Greenways' established by the City Council since 1983. There are four 'Greenways West Walks' in the Shirley Warren district, leading from Tanner's Brook in Dale Valley Road to Lordswood. They not only pro-vide areas of recreation but also preserve wildlife habitats and enhance Southampton's landscape.

Further Reading

Nicholson, Paul *A Photographic History of Southampton General Hospital*, Shirley Press, 1990.

Southampton Schools Conservation Corps *Greenways in Southampton*, Southampton City Council, 1993.

Wilkinson, Rosaleen *Millbrook, The Hidden Past*, R. Wilkinson, 2002.

Williams, Robert *Herbert Collins 1885–1975*, Paul Cave Publications, 1985.

Woodcock, Lloyd *Aldermoor, 1938–89*, Aldermoor School, 1990.

Sholing

including Botany Bay, Sholing Common and Weston Common

THERE are various explanations for the origin of the name Sholing, spelt 'Scholing' on many old maps. One version is that it means, in Old English, 'the hill above the shore' or 'the hill sloping down to the shore' and it is true that Sholing is indeed on high ground and slopes down towards Southampton Water. However, others think that the ending '-ing' indicates an area where the sons of a man named 'Schol' lived. The Old English 'Sceolingas' means 'people associated with somebody called Sceolh', a nickname for somebody who was crooked or squint-eyed. Another local Romany explanation is that it comes from the presence of heather, or 'ling', and the phrase a 'nice show o' ling'. This rather fanciful explanation can, I think, be discounted.

The area is also known locally as Spike Island, for which there are various explanations. One is that it originates from the heathland's characteristic spiky gorse that still springs up whenever a piece of open land is left unattended. Another quite unfounded suggestion is that it stems from the spikes that secured the chains of convicts held in the area prior to being transported to Australia.

The most likely explanation lies in the former penal colony of Inis Pich, translated as Spike Island – a small island off Cork Harbour, Ireland. This was used in the time of Cromwell to hold Irish rebels and in the 19th century deportees were despatched from the colony to Botany Bay in Australia. It is perhaps no coincidence that part of Sholing, still inhabited by descendents of travellers and gypsies, is called 'Botany Bay' to this day.

Bronze tools have been found east of the Itchen and there are many burial mounds, or tumuli, in the area. An 1810 map depicts one on Sholing Common. The earliest mention of Sholing, however, is in 1251, when Henry III granted it to the Abbot of Netley Abbey. Another reference to it is contained in the Register of the nearby Priory Church of St Andrew, Hamble, where, in 1679, it refers to 'Sholin'. A further entry, in 1795, states 'There are two hundred and forty souls in this parish, in Sholing 43…' The area was then rather desolate, mainly gorse land and heather, and was part of the Parish of Hound, which also included nearby Hamble and Bursledon. The undeveloped Sholing Common was used as a holding area for troops awaiting embarkation in the late 18th and early 19th-century wars with France. It was home to a Volunteer Rifle Range in the 1880s, recalled in the local road names of Butts Road, Dragoon Close, Shooters Hill Close and the local public house, The Target.

Several factors contributed to changing the character of the small country villages east of the Itchen, the first being the inauguration of the Floating Bridges across the River Itchen in 1836, coupled with the construction of Southampton Docks in 1840. The resultant creation of the road to Portsmouth made the entire district more accessible, adjoining, as it did, the Woolston and Itchen areas. The latter had become fashionable for the gentry, who wanted to get away from the rapidly developing industrial area of Southampton and live in the nearby countryside.

Sholing never existed as a village but a small hamlet of brick bungalow-type cottages were built in the 1790s in the Botany Bay Road area.

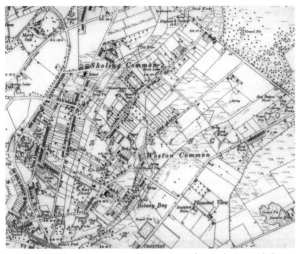

1911 map of Sholing. Note the number of gravel pits and the absence of housing in the northeast section. *(Reproduced from the 1911 Ordnance Survey map. NC/03/17894)*

The first inhabitants were poor and of Romany background. Many of them retained their caravans and they formed their own tight-knit community, one that continues to this day. These gypsy families would spend the winter in houses, with their caravans in the garden, and travel away in summer hop picking or fruit picking. The men would also race their horses on the local roads during their regular horse sales, to the great pleasure of the villagers and extreme frustration of the local Police, who rarely managed to outwit the frantic riders.

The opening of Netley Hospital in 1863 also created a need for housing for the hospital staff, and many came to live in Sholing, together with the servants and tradesmen who served the gentry. Buildings and new roads spread throughout the area and the new residents' spiritual needs were soon served by a Primitive Methodist Chapel, erected in 1856 at a cost of £106 and capable of seating 120 persons.

Sholing was ideal territory for the predominantly working-class dissenting Primitive Methodists at this time, with its high proportion of labourers. The main local industries were brick making, well digging (with everybody either owning or sharing a well), and strawberry growing. There were six brickyards scattered about the area, their presence revealed at night by the fires glowing in the kilns and clamps. Many inhabitants were in service, went to sea as stokers or stewards, or laboured in the docks, and their wives frequently took in laundry, often working together. Donkeys were a common form of transport for the numerous laundries and for the pedlars who carried out a thriving trade in the district. This gave rise to yet another nickname for the area, Donkey Common!

The established church soon followed and the Parish Church of St Mary's was consecrated in 1866. It is noteworthy that their first Vicar, the

A Primitive Methodist Chapel Anniversary tea party in South East Road, *c*.1908. 'Grannie', with her black bonnet and shawl, seated to the right of the picture, typifies the apparent accelerated ageing process of the time. She was almost certainly far younger than her appearance suggests. *(Dorothy Prior)*

The same view in 2004. The Chapel was demolished in 1982 and replaced by terraced houses. The Southern Gas Board had purchased the building for £13,750 in 1968 and used it as a store, but no doubt sold the site to developers for a good profit. The 'Tin Chapel' has been replaced by housing.

The Primitive Methodist 'Green's Chapel' in South East Road in 1908. William Thomas Musselwhite, a local builder and Trustee, built it in 1876 at a cost of £820. The two young lads in the foreground are delivering bread for Newburys Bakery from their shop on the corner of Bay Road and Kathleen Road. In the left background is the Plymouth Brethren 'Tin Chapel' in Chapel Crescent. *(Dorothy Prior)*

The 'Happy Shopper' in North East Road, just prior to its demolition in early 2000. Owned and run by Tom McEniry for many years, it was a good example of a small shopkeeper who was part of the community as well as providing a much-needed local service. Sadly, such small businesses are now few and far between.

The march of time has resulted in many small shops falling victim to the developer, as is the case here. The Happy Shopper site in 2004 is now home to at least four families – such is progress!

Revd Francis Davidson, remained in place for the next 48 years. Not to be outdone, the Primitive Methodists' growing popularity was demonstrated by the building of an impressive new chapel in nearby South-East Road in 1876. It soon became known as Green's Chapel, George Green being the most dynamic and forceful leading member of their congregation. The only known education in the area at that time was in a National School, Sholing Common, on the site of what is now the Salvation Army Hall, North-East Road, with children of all ages crowded into one classroom.

However, this improved when the National School for Girls and Infants was built in 1871, Sholing having increased to 1,444 inhabitants. It was directly opposite Sholing Church, in what was then Church Road, now St Monica Road. New buildings for 219 boys were also constructed in 1885 in Middle Road, and Sholing Infants School was built nearby in 1911. The following year the girls and infants of St Monica Road School exchanged premises with the boys

Sholing Temperance Band in 1912. Rear row, standing, are: G. Armstrong, A. Carter, G. Harding, G. Green, C. Fanner, F. Fanner, F. Reed, G.S. Clark, W. Durham, G. Benning and F. Parker. Sitting are: S. White, W. Green, A. Parker, C. Green, B. Long, J. Butt, W. Hannam, H. Taylor, L. Pearson and L. Veal. Sitting in front: H. Parker, N. Parker, B. Long and C. Baker.

Middle Road c.1910, looking north from the Baptist Chapel, built 1887, to the Robin Hood Public House. The Chapel retains a thriving membership and continues to be an important part of the local community. *(Bitterne Local History Society)*

of Middle Road and St Monica became a Boys' School. Following a number of temporary changes during World War Two, a new Junior School was built in St Monica Road in 1977 and the original building reverted to an Infants School.

At the turn of the century Sholing was surrounded by five toll gates, the Floating Bridge; Northam Bridge; Lances Hill, Hedge End and Bursledon Bridge. The only toll-free exit meant a journey through Bitterne via Mousehole to the

South East Road, c.1908, near the junction with Middle Road, opposite what used to be the Robin Hood public house, now the Earl of Locksley. The general shop on the right corner, with the letterbox in the wall and the Nestles Milk advert, was owned by the Misses R.E. & M. Barnes. Further down the road, also with a Nestles Milk and Viking Milk advert, was a small shop managed by Mrs L. Bennet. *(Dorothy Prior)*

The same view in February 1993. Mrs Bennet's Newsagents, Tobacconists and Confectioners shop was run for many years by her well-known and popular son Len, until it was demolished in early 1993 to make space for Sholing Girls' School playing fields. The first pair of houses left standing in the picture are today's Sholing Television and Charlie's Hairdressers premises. *(Joan Holt)*

Old cottages in North East Road, between Sholing Post Office and Cunningham Crescent, demolished in January 1991. These were typical 19th-century worker's cottages, common throughout the area but now, sadly, a rarity. The occupants were engaged in either agricultural work or in service, and many of the wives took in washing. A well would be shared between two or more houses. *(Joan Holt)*

Itchen Grammar School *c.*1960, viewed from the playing fields. It now has a well-equipped Sports & Performing Arts Centre that opened in 1998, with staff specialising in a very wide range of activities. The school also has a high reputation for music, with many pupils who are members of Southampton and Hampshire Orchestras. One notable Old Issonian was William Whitlock, born 1918, MP for Nottingham, former Comptroller of HM Household and Lord Commissioner of the Treasury. He was Parliamentary Secretary of State at the Foreign Office in 1968 and died in 2001. *(Joan Holt)*

free Cobden Bridge and this tended to make Sholing a rather isolated community.

However, in 1898 the parishes of St Mary Extra, Sholing and Hound were formed into Itchen Urban District, and this in turn was absorbed into the County Borough of Southampton in 1920, together with Bitterne and other areas east of the Itchen. The combined population of Bitterne and Sholing was then just under 10,000. This meant profound changes to the nature of all these areas, transforming their deeply entrenched rural attitudes.

A small railway station had been provided at the junction of Station Road and Cranbury Road in August 1866, with a single line, doubled in 1910, and with longer platforms. This proved to be of great value to the many local strawberry growers, market gardeners and brick makers and helped the area to prosper. Further business opportunities were created, such as Mr Darley's basket works in Spring Road, opposite Cranbury Road. This employed as many as 50 young women making baskets for the local fruit growers.

The railway line ran from Southampton to Fareham and on to Portsmouth, and this greatly improved their trading opportunities. Sadly, Sholing Station has been unstaffed since 1965 and in 1990 the old vandalised buildings were demolished and replaced by a waiting shelter.

Sholing did not suffer extensive damage during World War Two, although a number of houses were struck and a train standing between Sholing and Woolston received a direct hit, causing nine casualties. It was also the unwilling recipient of Southampton's first flying bomb, above the top of North-East Road on 12 July 1944, although fortunately there were no fatal casualties.

Extensive post-war council development was carried out, arising out of the urgent need to house the hundreds made homeless when large areas of the town were devastated during the many heavy blitzes. Council estates were developed between North-East and Kathleen Roads and between Butts Road and Botley Road, trans-

A 1905 view of Church Road, now St Monica Road, looking towards South East Road. In the background is the Salvation Army Hall, now the Elim Pentecostal Church, built in 1865 as Sholing's first Primitive Methodist Chapel. *(Dorothy Prior)*

In 2004 the passers-by posing for a photo are dressed differently to their counterparts of a century ago. Tracksuits and trainers now rule the day. Maxwell Road has now been built on the spot where they stand and the small front porch of the Elim Church can just be seen, with the rest now obscured by houses.

forming the former gravel pits, brickyards and market gardens into widespread residential areas.

Building a new Sholing Girls' School in Middle Road started in 1938, but because of wartime problems in obtaining building materials, and the evacuation of pupils, it was not taken into use until July 1945. During the war the girls were temporarily based in the nearby Merry Oak Boys' School, built in 1935, as well as in St Monica Road Boys' School. Sholing Girls' School completed its transition to a specialist College of Technology with an official ceremony in May 2003. This school is in the vanguard of advanced information technology, with sophisticated computer networking, wireless computers, laptops, video conferencing and interactive whiteboards.

Middle Road is also home to Itchen College, which started life in 1906 as a Pupil Teachers' Centre in Woolston. It later became Itchen Co-educational Secondary School and the transfer of the main body of the school to temporary huts on this Middle Road site took place in 1921, with the remainder using Station Road Elementary School. The foundation stone for the present building was laid in December 1925 but many factors, including a major fire, meant that it was not fully completed until 1938. During World War Two many pupils were evacuated to combine with Andover Grammar School and the school buildings were used as an ARP Post and Casualty Station with Medical Services. In June 1940 French troops who escaped from Dunkirk were given tea and sandwiches by the WRVS from the window of the Domestic Science room, but a British Restaurant was later established in the school dining hall.

The school became Itchen Grammar School in September 1946 and it is now Itchen College, one of the leading educational establishments east of the Itchen, with a reputation for being friendly, caring and innovative.

In 1961 the lovely scenic area of Miller's Pond, in the south-west corner of Sholing, was scheduled for massive development. The plans

Looking up Church Road, *c.*1905, from near the junction with Station Road, at the top of 'Brickyard Hill'. The unsurfaced road and pavements lead to the fork of what are now St Monica and Kathleen Roads. *(Dorothy Prior)*

The same view in 2004. The iron railings of the small front gardens were removed during World War Two as part of the war effort, and never replaced. Car parking is now a higher priority.

incorporated 700 houses, a new school, library and a shopping centre, but although the pond was culverted in 1965 the plans never came to fruition. It is now home to the Sholing Valley Study Centre, a very active voluntary environmental group with an interest in the local wildlife.

The current Sholing Council Ward population of over 15,500 is now an integral part of the City of Southampton, with little physical trace of its rural beginnings. But somehow it still manages to retain something of its former rustic charm, with its many open areas, albeit smaller than before, and its colourful gypsy characters.

Traces of its original rural nature have been retained through the network of Greenways established by the City Council since 1983. The three and a half mile long Shoreburs Greenway, from Weston Shore to Bursledon Road, runs through Sholing, with two routes linking at Miller's Pond. One runs between Middle Road and North-East Road, and the other between Kathleen Road and Butts Road. They are 'ribbons of open space which follow stream valleys' and preserve wildlife habitats. Sholing is fortunate to have these reminders of its rural past and long may they be retained.

Further Reading

Brown, Jim *The Story of St Andrew's Methodist Church, Sholing,* Sholing Press, 1995.
Hoare, Philip *Spike Island, The Memory of a Military Hospital,* Fourth Estate, 2001.
Local Studies Group, Southampton, *Woolston & Sholing,* 1984.
Malam, David *Learning From The Past,* Sholing Press, 1994.
Paynter, John *Bygone Days of Sholing,* Sholing Press, 1984.
—— *Memories of Old Sholing,* Sholing Press, 1991.
—— *Sholing, Past & Present,* Sholing Press, 1996.
Slade, Eileen *Change From Sixpence,* Southampton University, 1980.

St Denys

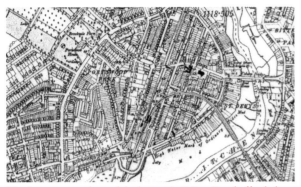

The long rear gardens of the houses in Priory Road afforded good access to the river in 1910, and still do, allowing the use of valuable private moorings. The wide sweep of the railway line, constructed in 1866 to bridge the Itchen and connect St Denys with Bitterne and the east, is very distinct. *(Reproduced from the 1910 Ordnance Survey map. NC/03/17894)*

IN 1120 news was brought to the Norman Henry I, who was said to be in Southampton Castle, of the drowning of his son Prince William off the coast of Normandy. Four years later the King founded a Priory for Augustine Canons on the outskirts of Southampton in his son's memory and dedicated it to St Denys, the patron saint of

In September 2002 Mrs Anna Jean Taylor of Redmond, Washington, US, paid a visit to St Denys to see where her great-grandfather, Captain Thomas Madden, and grandfather, also Thomas, lived at the end of the 19th century. She stands here at the remaining ruins of St Denys Priory, a spot where her grandfather would have played as a young boy. The family then lived in Priory House, demolished *c.*1905, which used to be directly opposite the ruins.

Paris. The monks were known as Black Canons, from their robes, and were instructed to always say a daily Mass in memory of Prince William.

The Priory was constructed on the west bank of the River Itchen, some three miles north of Southampton, and the King 'granted to God and the church of St Denys and the Canons serving there… a portion of land between Portswood and the Itchen', the rent of which was valued at 11s 6d per annum, and another parcel of land at Portswood giving a rental of 41s 6d.

Richard I later gave the Priory the entire Manor of Portswood and the Manor of Northam as well as a small church at Chilworth, which is still dedicated to St Denys. More gifts followed over the years, including, from Edward III in 1347, financial benefits, but also the care of the Leper Hospital on the Marlands (now the site of the Civic Centre) in Southampton. In spite of the many economic benefits the Priory received, it seems the Canons were nevertheless always suffering financial hardships.

For centuries the Canons followed their disciplined way of life, continued to say a mass for Prince William and were well liked by the local population. The days of the Priory, however, were numbered when Henry VIII gave orders for the Dissolution of the Monasteries. The King's Commissioners visited the Priory in 1536, when it was dissolved and the six remaining Canons had to leave. The buildings were then said to be in a state of 'extreme ruin and decay'.

Two years later the site, with the Manor of Portswood, was sold to Sir Francis Dawtrey, who lived in Tudor House in the town centre. The estate then passed through various hands and was purchased by the Earl of Peterborough, of Bevois Mount, in 1730. He, in turn, sold it to General Stibbert in 1776, who added it to his Portswood

St Denys Road *c*.1905, with St Denys School, opened 1882, on the right. The tram is en route to Cobden Bridge and will pass the site of the soon to be constructed Scala Picture House on its left, at the beginning of the bridge. The cinema was renamed the Lyric in 1926 and closed in 1940. *(Norman Gardiner Collection – Bitterne Local History Society)*

Park estate. The district remained an attractive country retreat during the heyday of Southampton's spa period, which had had come to an end by 1820.

However, in 1852 the entire estate was sold to developers and by 1861 roads had been laid out and a few houses constructed, half a dozen in Priory Road and just one in Adelaide Road. The old Priory buildings were still used by a Mr Skelton, partly as a home and partly as a farm. It was realised that St Denys would continue to grow and, with admirable foresight, it was decided to build a parish church. St Denys Church was consecrated in 1868, very close to the ancient Priory, thus continuing the Christian tradition. This church still has on show a stone coffin that came from the ruined Priory, together with a wall plaque displaying a number of floor tiles, some showing the fleur-de-lys, recovered from the ruins.

During this period further intensive building took place around the area and the Priory fell into ruin, with some of its stones used to build the strong stone wall that borders the nearby River Itchen. Fortunately, Mr R. E. Nicholas, the first curator of the Tudor House Museum, rescued a beautiful archway and erected it in the garden of Tudor House, where it can be seen to this day. One remaining fragment of wall still stands in the garden of a private house in Priory Road, and gives some idea of how substantial the full structure must have been.

The area changed somewhat when the railway first came to the area. A station was provided, which officially opened in 1861 and was called Portswood Station (renamed St Denys in 1876). As part of the construction of a line from Portswood to Netley in 1866, the track went through the area, with a railway bridge erected over the River Itchen from Priory Road.

Some idea of the nature of the early properties in this area can be gleaned from an article on Priory House (a former large farmhouse directly opposite the ruined Priory) that appeared in the

The Railway Hotel *c.*1899, on the corner of St Denys Road and Osborne Road. Built in the late 1860s, it was demolished in 1986 when the Thomas Lewis Way bypass was constructed. When this picture was taken it was owned by Coopers Brewery and Edward R. Woolford was the licensee. *(Henry Brain Collection – Maureen Webber)*

The same view in 2007.

Hampshire Magazine in December 1974. Captain Thomas Madden purchased this mansion between 1871 and 1881, when he moved there from Poole. (His great-grand-daughter, Mrs Anna Jean Taylor, currently lives in Redmond, Washington, US). The article, written by G.H. Manser, states:

> The house was a large, rambling old place with extensive, and to me some-what eerie, cellars and stabling, the latter much too spacious for my grandmother's one pony, Judy, who was an important member of the family when the trams came only to Portswood Junction. A large lawn with flower borders ran from the side of the house down to Priory Road. In the other direction the kitchen garden occupied the corner with St Denys Road at the bottom and Priory Road on one side. Here stood a large greenhouse, a vine house and many soft fruit bushes with apples, pears, cherries etc. and a patch of vegetables.

At the beginning of this century my grandmother sold two strips of land, one facing St Denys Road and the other facing Priory Road, and on these 13 houses were built. The ground floors of several in St Denys Road were later turned into shops. Two points I remember vividly. One was going out with my father before breakfast to be given a piece of a ripe green fig, which he had just cut from the fig tree that grew on the side of the house facing Priory Road – the flavour is with me yet. The other is playing with my brother in two stone coffins that lay under the trees at the bottom of the garden. They were supposed to have come from the Priory in earlier days and many were the ceremonies we enacted around

St Denys Road, at the corner of Belmont Road, *c.*1950. Fred Trim Ltd of 63–65 Oxford Street owns the fruit and vegetable lorry turning out of Belmont Road and Tram No.11 has made the long climb from Cobden Bridge on its way from Bitterne Park Triangle to the Docks. *(Norman Gardiner Collection – Bitterne Local History Society)*

and in the coffins. After my grand-mother's death in 1904 my aunt sold the house and it was demolished and other houses built on the site.

The district was transformed in 1883 when the National Liberal Land Company constructed the free Cobden Bridge across the River Itchen, joining Priory Road to Manor Farm Road at what is now known as Bitterne Park Triangle. The Company had purchased 317 acres of farmland on the eastern side of the river, scheduled for mas-sive development. When this was completed the bridge provided quick and easy access between the two districts and the City, opening up com-mercial advantages for both sides.

The area is now a peaceful suburb of the town, enjoying the benefits of shopping in adjacent Portswood and access to the east. It also has the advantages of the riverfront, where houseboats are moored and a well-maintained marina is managed by the long-established family firm of Dyer Brothers, Boatbuilders.

Further Reading

Brown, Jim *Bridging the Itchen*, Bitterne Local History Society, 2002.

Ticehurst, Brian *Sights & Scenes of St Denys*, B. & J. Ticehurst, 1991.

Swaythling

including Hampton Park, Mansbridge, Townhill Park and Woodmill

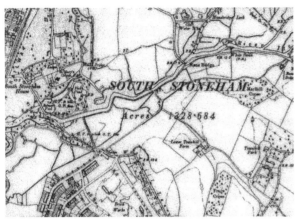

This 1910 map shows South Stoneham House in the east, just above Woodmill. Mans Bridge, spelt as two words, is on the River Itchen in the north, just before the White Swan public house, and Townhill Park is in the south-east. *(Reproduced from the 1910 Ordnance Survey map. NC/03/17894)*

South Stoneham House in 1914. Built for Edmond Dummer in 1708, it was purchased by William Sloane in 1735. His uncle, Sir Hans Sloane, formed the first collection that became the British Museum. (Sloane Square, Sloane Street and Hans Crescent in London are named after him.) The famous Capability Brown laid out the gardens some time after 1772. *(Peter Heard)*

IT IS difficult to determine the origin of this name, possibly hypothetical Old English 'SwaeÔeling', 'a place of mist'. A hamlet, with many varied spellings, most usually Swathling, was partially in the large parish of South Stoneham. The following is recorded in the 1086 Domesday Book, within the Mansbridge Hundred, and it gives some idea of the surrounding area at that time:

> The bishop himself holds Staneham. It is for the clothing of the monks. In the time of King Edward it was assessed at five hides; now at three hides. There is land for nine ploughs. In demesne is one plough; and 11 villans and nine bordars with eight ploughs. There is one slave, 23 acres of meadow and fisheries rendering 39d and woodland for 20 pigs. In the time of King Edward it was worth £7; and afterwards £4; now £8.

Other record books suggest that the original sparsely populated Swathling village, served by the 12th-century church of St Mary's, South Stoneham, was along the ford close to where the modern Fleming Arms now stands. However, the scattered thatched cottages had a new neighbour in 1708 when South Stoneham House was built for Edmond Dummer and an important new owner by 1895 was Sir Samuel Montagu, the senior partner of a London banking firm. He became Baron Swaythling in 1907 and was a prominent figure in the area for many years.

Local education was catered for by Swaythling School, in Mayfield Road, opened in 1898 when the area was still a village with numerous fields and farms. It was initially planned to accommodate 150 children, packed 50 to a class. Built at a cost of £902, plus £74 for a protecting fence, it was on land donated by Catherine Corey. By 1930, with the massive increase of housing in the area, the number of children had grown to 694,

A late 19th-century view of old cottages between Halfpenny's Corner and Swaythling Railway Bridge, at what is now the entrance of the Thomas Lewis Way bypass. The beginning of the footbridge to Swaythling Station, opened in 1883, can just be seen at the extreme left of the picture. *(Norman Gardiner Collection – Bitterne Local History Society)*

The same view in 2004, with the buildings swept away in the course of constructing the wider road and the bypass.

so the following year a new Senior School, now Hampton Park School, was completed, adjoining Swaythling School.

Fred Woolley, an accountant and local politician; Claude Ashby, a businessman and youth club enthusiast; and Herbert Collins, the well-known architect, formed the Swaythling Housing Society in 1925. This society was the first such society in the Southampton area and its initial development was in Pilgrim Place, with terraced houses and flats built around three sides of a central green and the existing trees retained. The Society's ambitious building programme contin-

ued throughout the area, using its own workforce to keep costs low, and the income from rents and a few sales to maintain momentum. Herbert Collins was the principal designer and by 1936 a total of 110 houses had been built to create Monks Way and Brookside Way.

The Society then extended its interest beyond Swaythling into various areas of the town, a process that continues to the present day. Its headquarters is at Northleigh Corner, Wide Lane, aptly named 'Herbert Collins House' after the individual who gave Swaythling so much of its present character. Absorbed into the borough in 1920, it

Langhorn Road at the junction with Burgess Street (Road), leading down to Portswood Road/High Road and the junction with Woodmill Lane, c.1909. This view of the initial odd-numbered houses in Langhorn Road would now be obscured by the even-numbered houses built on the opposite side of the road. *(Norman Gardiner Collection – Bitterne Local History Society)*

also embraces Mansbridge, Woodmill and Townhill Park.

The ancient bridge at Mansbridge was the only road link across the River Itchen in the vicinity of Southampton and the sole north-eastern road exit from the town for centuries. The date of its original construction is lost in the mists of time, but theories abound. Parts of the Roman road that led south from Winchester are still visible, until it enters modern Stoneham, near Mansbridge, to which it is heading in a straight line.

The Saxon word 'man(e)bri(c)g' is said to mean the meeting place of a man or men, or bridge or causeway. It was mentioned by name as early as 932, in King Athelstan's Charter to the Prior of St Swithun, but it is not known whether or not a bridge existed at that time. It could equally well have been a ford crossing point. The 11th-century Domesday Book also records the Manor of Manebrige or 'Manesbrige' on the

The shop blind is out on Pritchett's Bakery, High Road, near the corner of Burgess Street, in 1908. The Hampton Park Hotel, renamed the Old Black Cat in 1991, was built in 1924 on the vacant plot just beyond the row of buildings and is now a McDonald's restaurant. *(Norman Gardiner Collection – Bitterne Local History Society)*

The same view in 2004, with the ubiquitous McDonald's at the bottom of Burgess Road.

Itchen and on 20 September 1332 Edward III, when confirming earlier gifts of land, included two acres of meadow land in Manebrig. This main east/west road system to the north of Southampton would require any possible bridge at Mansbridge to be maintained and rebuilt as necessary. This is shown by a 1403 record in *Wykeham's Registers* that indulgence for a period of 40 days was granted to persons subscribing 'to

The existing disused little hump-backed bridge in the foreground, with its single tooled stone arched span of 30ft and headroom of 5ft 10in, is said to have been built by John Doswell Doswell (yes, the surname *is* duplicated) in the early 19th century on the site of an earlier bridge. He was surveyor to the Town Council, the Waterworks and the Harbour & Pier Commissioners and designed the Royal Pier, opened by the Duchess of Kent, accompanied by her 14-year-old daughter Princess Victoria, on 8 July 1833. The modern bridge behind it is a pre-stressed concrete structure, opened to road traffic in the summer of 1975. It has a single span of about 100ft, minimum headroom of about 10ft and carries the now heavy traffic of the A27.

The River Itchen at Mansbridge in 1908, with the White Swan Hotel in the background. This opened at the beginning of the 19th century as the Middleton Arms, named after the family who then owned most of the nearby Townhill Park Estate. Changed to the Swan Inn by 1830 and the Swan Hotel in 1870, it is now a popular carvery. *(Norman Gardiner Collection – Bitterne Local History Society)*

repair the highway at Mannsbrigge, leading to Southampton'.

An early 19th-century bridge at this spot served Southampton and the surrounding area well for many years and although replaced by a modern highway just to the north-east it remains as a reminder of the original ancient route to the east.

The nearby site of Woodmill, also on the Itchen, is that of an ancient corn mill and in 1781 Walter Taylor, a manufacturer of wood blocks, transferred his business there from Weston Mill (recently partially excavated in Mayfield Park). The stream at Weston had not been able to supply enough water to drive his mill in the summer months and this problem did not exist to anything like the same degree at Woodmill. Walter built new and bigger workshops and erected a rotative steam engine to drive the large circular saw he is credited with having invented.

He also had a virtual monopoly on supplying wooden rigging blocks to the Royal Navy, his success being very much due to his technical innovations. He was one of the pioneers of mass production methods, using movable stops and formers for fast and accurate production of rigging blocks, which had a consequent reputation for being very reliable. The Taylor water mill burned down in 1820 and there is little or no trace of the buildings that housed the steam-driven machinery. It was replaced by a flour mill in the 19th century and acquired in the 1960s by Southampton City Council Education Committee. It is now used as a Sailing and Canoeing Centre.

The adjoining River Itchen was probably navigable as far as Winchester during the Roman occupation of Clausentum, but it was allowed to fall into disrepair. Godfrey de Lucy, Bishop of Winchester from 1189 to 1204, was responsible for making the river navigable again, not just between Southampton and Winchester but also as far as Alresford. Unfortunately it appears that

Woodmill, as a 19th-century working flour mill. A modern asphalt road has now, of course, replaced the Woodmill wooden bridge and it is hard to believe that this area, with its narrow turns and single-way traffic, was once part of an important waterborne through route to Winchester and beyond. *(Bitterne Local History Society)*

lack of regular maintenance once again gradually rendered the river more and more difficult to use.

An attempt was made in 1665 to revitalise this useful form of transportation by an Act of Parliament that authorised improvements on a number of rivers, including the Itchen. A group of seven people were empowered to restore navigation for 'Boats, Barges, Lighters and other Vessels to the Itchin or Itching'. In return for their investment and work the seven Grantees were allowed to operate a monopoly on the carriage of goods upon the waterway.

Thus was born the Itchen Navigation, an improved existing river as opposed to a newly constructed canal. It necessitated making alterations to the banks and bed of existing parts of the river, improving irrigation channels and making new excavations to form canal links and thus shorten some of the winding sections. The water was retained by locks throughout its length, although the mill owners and owners of water meadows competed for its supply.

It proved to be a lengthy process, with a number of lawsuits and other conflicts with landowners and millers delaying the work, and the full length was not finally completed until 1710. The most important traffic on the Itchen Navigation was coal, shipped from the north-east coast by collier brigs and trans-shipped into barges at Northam Wharf for delivery to Winchester. In order to pass under low bridges barges travelling downstream frequently carried chalk or similar material as ballast.

From 1839 onwards the barge traffic on the Itchen had to compete with the new steam traction system of the London and Southampton Railway. Despite all their efforts the declining commercial traffic finally petered out in 1869 and the Itchen Navigation gradually slipped back into decay. There is perhaps a degree of hope for its future, as the Itchen Navigation Society was formed in 1976 and among its aims is the eventual restoration and conservation of the entire Navigation.

The last barge to carry a cargo to Winchester tied up at Blackbridge Wharf in June 1869, loaded with coal. The site of the lock at Woodmill is still apparent, although somewhat obscured by modern developments. This sea lock was reconstructed in 1829, with two pairs of gates retaining the water, but with a third pair pointing downstream to prevent salt water flowing into the Navigation at high spring tides. Even after the cessation of the main line traffic, Woodmill lock remained in use for barges going up the mainstream to the mill at West End. A wooden bridge,

A view of Woodmill from South Stoneham House in 1990. The houses in Oliver Road have valuable private moorings on the upper reach of the River Itchen and the spacious grounds of the aptly named Riverside Park provide a wonderful recreation area.

15 feet wide and set at an angle of 40 degrees to the line of the lock chamber gave access over it. It is thought that this was constructed around 1710, when the Itchen Navigation was finally completed, thus forming, with the nearby bridge at Mansbridge, a second means of travelling over the river.

The nearby Manor of Townhill was among the lands granted by Henry VIII in 1536 to Sir William Paulet after the Dissolution of the Monasteries. There is otherwise little recorded of the area, which was undoubtedly mainly used for farming. Nathaniel Middleton, who bought the land now known as Townhill Park in around 1787, was a 'Nabob': somebody who had made his fortune in the service of the East India Company, usually by enhancing their salary with gratuities, commissions and private trading. He enlarged the farmhouse, which burnt down, and in 1793 he built the nucleus of Townhill Park House.

Later owned by the Gater family, it was purchased by Sir Samuel Montagu (later Baron Swaythling) of South Stoneham House around 1897 and considerably enlarged and re-faced in the 'Italian villa' style by the second Lord Swaythling. However, it was decided that the house was too expensive to maintain and it was sold in 1948, with 30 acres, to Middlesex County Council. The remainder of the 324-acre estate was sold to Southampton Borough Council, who developed what is now the Townhill Park Estate, a mix of council and private properties.

The building was acquired by the City Council in 1969 and in 1971 became a student hostel for 75 marine cadets. Because of a decline in the number of merchant ships and falling student numbers it was sold to the independent Gregg School in 1994. This started in the town with 180 pupils on secretarial courses and is now a mixed school of 345 pupils who are taught the National Curriculum. The beautiful gardens are still maintained and are well worth a visit on the Gregg School regular Open Days.

The dominant industry in Swaythling is the 44-acre complex of the Ford Motor Company in Wide Lane. They acquired the site in 1958

Townhill Park House in the 21st century. Gertrude Jekyll, the famous garden designer, laid out the wonderful gardens that were particularly noted for their rhododendrons, azaleas and camellias, all of which thrived on the acid soil. A staff of about 25 highly skilled gardeners lovingly maintained the gardens that were much admired by Queen Mary, wife of George V. *(Vince Davies)*

and began producing vehicles in 1961. A £74 million investment programme in 1985 made it the most modern in Europe, with state-of-the-art computerised robot equipment carrying out three quarters of the welding and with advanced machine monitoring equipment. Its main product has been the Ford Transit, turning out more than half of the country's production: a far cry from the sleepy rural area of the not too distant past.

Further Reading

Allen, Jack *Swaythling, More Than a Fleeting Glance,* J. Allen, 1994.

Brown, Jim *Bridging the Itchen,* Bitterne Local History Society, 2002.

Coney, Ralph and Brown, Jim *Townhill Park House,* Bitterne Local History Society, 1999.

Harrison, Geoffrey *To Be A Farmer's Boy,* G. Harrison, 1997.

Mann, John Edgar *The Book of the Stonehams,* Halsgrove, 2002.

Ticehurst, Brian *Sights & Scenes of Swaythling,* B. & J. Ticehurst, 1998.

Williams, Robert *Herbert Collins 1885–1975,* Paul Cave Publications, 1985.

Thornhill
including Hightown and Thornhill Park

FROM 252 feet above sea level, almost the highest point in the City, Thornhill, with its sub-district of Hightown, drops gently south-eastwards, the fall being broken only by the shallow transverse valley of a now piped stream. Its name is self-explanatory and a 19th-century writer described the main roadway in this area as 'dull and monotonous, barren heath'. It was then largely isolated and uninhabited, with little trace of the Roman road that had crossed it en route to Portchester and Chichester. The heathlands in the eastern section, known as Netley Common, were used as temporary military camping grounds and an army under the command of the Earl of Moira is known to have camped there in 1794, en route to Ostend via Botley.

A combination of circumstances prompted proposals for new road construction during this period. The Industrial Revolution created a demand for more and larger vehicles, with consequently better roads, and the military had need of good direct routes to embark on ships at Southampton or Portsmouth. At the same time men of substance were developing great estates east of the River Itchen and the Northam and Bursledon bridges, giving direct access to the east, were constructed by 1800. Development eastwards from Bitterne soon followed.

For centuries most of the area had been part of South Stoneham Parish, with the south-western remainder in St Mary Extra Parish. By the time of the 1815 enclosure award the South Stoneham portion was awarded to William Hallett, Lord of the Manor of 'Townhill otherwise Shamblehurst', and the St Mary Extra part to William Chamberlayne, MP. William Cobbett of Botley, champion of the poor and author of *Rural Rides* (1830) was a friend of William Chamberlayne and crossed the heaths to visit him at Weston Grove. Other parts of the area were common land with no acknowledged owner.

In 1825 Michael Hoy, a prosperous London merchant, purchased a large piece of land and a farmhouse in Shamblehurst. He erected a large mansion high on its south-east facing slope but died before its completion. The property was left to his second cousin, James Barlow, who then

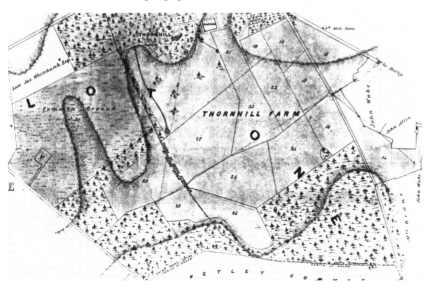

Plan of Lot One of the Thornhill Farm Estate 'to be sold by auction by Mr George Robins at the Auction Mart, London, on Thursday June 13th 1844, at 12 o'clock in three lots.' Thornhill Farm had 430 acres of land, with significant farm buildings at the north-east but what appears to be a pair of houses above the word Thornhill, served by a lodge to its north. The modern Thornhill Estate, of course, now replaces the agricultural land and woods. *(Bitterne Local History Society)*

131

Thornhill Park House *c.*1910. The Mansion, built in the Italian style, was constructed of white bricks, partly stuccoed, on massive vaults with a slated roof and a 170-foot colonnade on the south façade. There were five large reception rooms, 18 bedrooms with five more for the staff, two large halls, a gunroom, billiard room and a ballroom. It was surrounded by kitchen and children's gardens, rhododendrons, specimen trees and shrubs, croquet and tennis lawns and a vinery. *(Keith Le May)*

A 2003 view, from the south-west, of what was the front elevation of Thornhill Park House. The photo was taken from Thornhill Avenue and shows No.33 on the left. The building stretched as far as Cowper Road on the right.

added Hoy to his name. His aunt remained at the mansion until her death in 1839, whereupon Barlow Hoy moved into the building, with its 200 acres, which he called Thornhill Park.

James Barlow Hoy was also Tory MP for Southampton and a benefactor. He was accidentally killed while hunting in the Pyrenees in 1843 and there is a monument to him in West End church. The estate land north of the modern Thornhill Park Road was then woodland, mainly firs, which screened the mansion from the north winds.

Henry Dumbleton, aged 63, purchased the estate in 1846. He had joined the East India Company in 1799, rising from clerk to judge. The farmhouse then housed the bailiff, head carter and head gardener. Two parts of the terrace remain. They are close to the junction of Thornhill Park Road with Kanes Hill Roundabout and can be seen from Simon Way. They are notable for their tall and ornate brick chimney stacks.

The 1851 census shows that a housekeeper, butler, young ladies' maid, cook, housemaid, and under housemaid were living in, with the coachman and his wife living in the nearby lodge. Dumbleton rented land bordering Sholing Common from the Chamberlaynes. This is now

the site of Thornhill School, its playing fields and adjacent roads. Dumbleton, whose name is perpetuated in the modern Dumbleton Towers block of flats, died in 1877, aged 94, and is buried at the rear of Bitterne churchyard.

Dumbleton's successor was Colonel Frank Willan, a young officer with a great love of the water who bought the property to be near boats and the yachting fraternity. He bred and maintained a herd of prize-winning Jersey cows and devoted considerable energy to local community work. He was keenly interested in the welfare of the sick and Willan Ward in the Royal South Hants Hospital is named after him. Of his six children, three went to Eton, one becoming a Brigadier General and another a Brigadier. Willan was so keen on shooting that he constructed a range in his grounds, where all his children were taught to shoot, boys and girls alike.

He sold Thornhill Park in 1910 to John Norman Campbell, a retired Ceylon tea planter, who died in 1916. His widow, a fine pianist and sportswoman, sold the estate, which by then comprised some 430 acres, to Ernest Travis, a timber merchant, in 1923. He was only interested in the standing timber and after its clearance an agent sold the land by lots, the largest purchaser being William Candy, whom Candy Lane commemorates.

The house, which stood between the present

The view from the top of Thornhill Park House in 1910, looking south towards the Solent, shows just how peaceful and unspoilt the estate was at that time. The landed gentry enjoying the view did not dream that within a few decades it would be transformed into a vast council estate with well over 11,000 residents. *(Keith Le May)*

Thornhill Avenue and Cowper Road, just north of Byron Road, was demolished in 1927. Two lodges stood in Thornhill Park Road, one at the top of Thornhill Avenue, demolished in the 1960s and the other, still standing, at the junction of Thornhill Park Road and Upper Deacon Road. Just off the latter and just outside the estate, is the Victorian house 'Thornfield', formerly occupied by a Colonel Bucknill. Much disguised by modern 'improvements' it is now home to the Royal British Legion.

A 32-year-old Australian character arrived on the scene in 1924, Herbert John Louis Hinkler, who bought a piece of land at the southern end of the estate where he built his house, 'Mon Repos'. Known as 'Bert' he is remembered for the first solo flight to Australia, in an Avro Avian single-seater plane in February 1928. However, he was killed in 1933 when trying to repeat his success and the winding spine of Hinkler Road, in the well-landscaped estate, commemorates this internationally known personality.

It was not until the turn of the 20th century that Hightown appeared on maps, at the extreme south-east of the suburb. In 1914 the Itchen Urban District Council earmarked part of this area for an isolation hospital, but this was not pursued.

Housebuilding along Thornhill Park Road began in the 1920s, but the road was not surfaced

Deacon and Upper Deacon Roads, *c.*1925, looking towards Thornhill Park Road, before the crossing with Bursledon Road was staggered. Formerly Thornhill Road and once known as Furzey Lane, this area was also known as 'Sheepwash', perhaps dating from when sheep had to be dipped on their way to Southampton market. It was also the site of a well-known small brickyard. *(Bitterne Local History Society)*

The Ladies Walk at Thornhill, so called because the gates of Thornhill Estate were opened on Sundays to allow ladies to use it as a short cut to West End Church. This entrance, now built on, was in Thornhill Park Road directly opposite the junction with Thornhill Avenue. *(Bitterne Local History Society)*

The lodge to Thornhill Park Estate, at the junction of what is now Thornhill Park Road and Upper Deacon Road. One of two in that road, the other was halfway along Thornhill Park Road, opposite the site of the former Post Office. *(Keith Le May)*

until 1929, when the County Council took over responsibility. 'Bungalow Town', immediately to the south, came next, with the builders beginning the local fashion for naming roads after poets. Street lighting arrived in 1934 but mains drainage was not provided until after World War Two.

In 1954, with Southampton needing more land to house its growing population, it succeeded in extending its boundaries to include all but a nar-row strip of the old Thornhill Park Estate. Plans were drawn up to house 11,000 people and to provide schools, public houses, a church and other social amenities. The policy of naming roads after literary personalities continued, but Tennyson Road became Farringford Road (after the poet's Isle of Wight residence) to avoid confu-

Thornhill Park Stores – later the Post Office. The sign states that it provided teas, ices and minerals and the boards on the pavement advertise Players Weights and Wills Star cigarettes, brands long vanished. *(Bitterne Local History Society)*

A more recent view of the former Lodge to the Thornhill Park Estate at the top of Upper Deacon Road, c.1995. The right portion is a modern extension. *(Bitterne Local History Society)*

The Victorian Thornfield House, at the end of Windover Close, leading from Upper Deacon Road. Formerly the home of Lt.Col. John Townsend Bucknill, RE, it is now home to the Royal British Legion. It had large tennis courts and an impressive garden, tended by Jim Emery, the Head Gardener.

Thornhill Stores in Thornhill Park Road, c.1938, with several of the units standing empty. All the shops were completed and occupied by the outbreak of war in 1939. *(Bitterne Local History Society*

Joan Holt stands outside the reconstructed 'Mon Repos', 29 Lydgate Road, the former home of Bert Hinkler. When it was threatened with demolition in 1982 it was carefully dismantled by a group of aviation enthusiasts and rebuilt in Bundaberg, his hometown in Queensland. It is now the Hinkler Museum and the focus of the town's Botanic Gardens. *(Joan Holt)*

sion with the road of that name in Portswood.

Many of the initial properties were designed or approved by the renowned architect, Herbert Collins, and are of a high standard. Others are council properties, some semi-detached and others in tower blocks. In 2003 the sum of £21 million, from government grants and council funds, was allocated to improve the Thornhill area's 2,200 council houses to 'bring them up to decent homes standard'. Nearly £10,000 is being spent on each home, upgrading the kitchen, bathroom and communal areas.

The end result will be an improvement to an already large thriving housing estate. The former farm, woodlands, heathland and grand estate have been lost to homes and roads, but nevertheless the area retains its own special identity.

Further Reading

Bitterne Local History Society *Bitterne Before the By-Pass*, Sholing Press, 1991.
—— *Images of England – Bitterne*, Tempus Publishing, 1999.
Pilson, Irene *Memories of Bitterne*, Kingfisher Railway Productions, 1984.
—— *More Memories of Bitterne*, Biddles Ltd, 1988.
Williams, Robert *Herbert Collins 1885–1975*, Paul Cave Publications, 1985.

Weston
including Mayfield

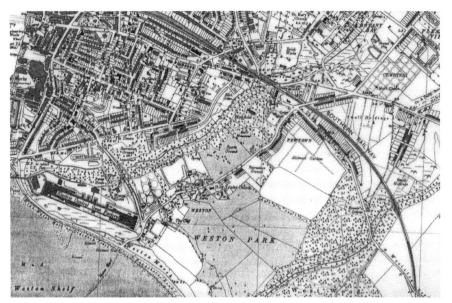

Weston Grove House (demolished *c.*1940) is just visible above the 'Electric Control Gear Factory', generally known as the Rolling Mills, in this 1939 map. The Mayfield Estate is in the north and Weston Park is now a large sprawling estate with striking tower blocks on the shoreline. *(Reproduced from the 1939 Ordnance Survey map. NC/03/17894)*

THE name of this district, on the extreme southeast shore of Southampton, could possibly come from the Old English 'west tun', meaning 'west farm or settlement', i.e. relative to the nearby Hampshire village of Old Netley and its adjacent West Wood. The earliest known reference to what was then a very small village, dependent on fishing and farming, is found in an Anglo-Saxon Charter of Ethelred (979–1013) that mentions lands 'in loco qui appellatur Westun' – a place called Westun.

By 1332 we read of John de Weston, a Burgess of Parliament for Southampton, but little else is known of the area until 1617 when a complaint was made by the Southampton Town Clerk about the 'fishermen of Weston dredging for oysters within the haven'. The relative importance of this fishing village was shown in 1756 when jurors from Weston were summoned to an Admiralty Court at nearby Hamble to confer on fishing rights.

In about 1770 Thomas Dummer of Woolston House sold the land around northern Weston Lane to Walter Taylor (1734–1803). It contained a small stream, fed by nearby Millers Pond, that ran along the western edge of Mayfield Park. Taylor built a mill and workshops to manufacture his specialist wood blocks for the Royal Navy, and modern excavations on the site have revealed details of their foundations. However, the water supply was sporadic and by 1782 he had moved to Woodmill.

Thomas Dummer died in 1781 and his lifelong friend, William Chamberlayne, inherited his estates, including what was then marked on maps as Weston Park. William, who died in 1799, was a descendant of Count John de Tankerville who arrived on these shores with William the Conqueror. Chamberlayne's son, also William, built a villa he called Weston Grove on the estate in 1802, where he entertained such notables as William Cobbett, the celebrated writer of *Rural Rides*, and Sir William Hamilton, husband of Lord Nelson's famous mistress.

Chamberlayne was extremely active in civic

Erected in 1802 by William Chamberlayne, Weston Grove House was just to the west of today's Archery Road and south of Swift Gardens. It was described in the local guidebook as 'an elegant mansion on a delightful spot, commanding a pleasant view of the river, Isle of Wight, Calshot Castle, New Forest etc'. The grounds were bordered by Weston Lane in the east and stretched as far north as the modern Wright's Hill.

The River Itchen shoreline at Woolston, looking towards Northam and the town, c.1802. The docks and floating bridges are conspicuous by their absence, and the spires of St Michael's and Holy Rood Churches are clearly visible. This idyllic rural setting is in the vicinity of the bottom of Swift Road and was undoubtedly part of William Chamberlayne's Weston Grove Estate. *(Joy Plummer)*

The Upper and Lower Arches in Weston Lane c.1905. The two arches were constructed across Weston Lane by William Chamberlayne to form a circuit, so he could ride in his carriage across both sections of his estate. This was after Weston Grove House was built in 1802. The estate covered the entire length of Weston Lane, as far as Wright's Hill. The upper arch was demolished in 1931 and the lower arch (through which the Sun Hotel can just be seen) in 1948. *(Henry Brain Collection – Maureen Webber)*

affairs and was one of Southampton's MP's from 1818 until his death in 1829. As chairman of the gas company that supplied the town he donated the iron columns for its new gas streetlights (with perhaps some vested interest?) and in 1822, as a tribute, the residents subscribed to a magnificent 50-foot cast-iron column. After a number of moves, it stands today, nicely refurbished, at the Hanover Buildings entrance to Houndwell Park, at the beginning of the fine avenue of lime trees planted by Sir Frederick Perkins during his mayoralty in 1862.

Chamberlayne was known as a generous employer, paying his labourers 13 shillings a week, compared to the eight shillings paid by many other landowners. Following his death in 1831 the estate passed to his cousin, Thomas Chamberlayne, a yacht-racing enthusiast whose yacht *Arrow* won the America's Cup in 1851. When Thomas died in 1876, his younger son, Tankerville, carried on the yachting tradition as well as

A peaceful meandering village Weston Lane, leading to the sea at Weston Shore, *c.*1904. The Sun Hotel on the left dates from the 1830s. In the early 20th century it belonged to Scrase's Star Brewery but it has been a Whitbread house since 1969. *(Bill White)*

The scene has changed by 2004, but the Sun Hotel has survived and remains a popular venue.

the ancient family name. (Tankerville's elder brother, Denzil, who took part in the famous charge of the Light Brigade at Balaclava, had died without an heir in 1873.) Tankerville was the Conservative MP for Southampton for many years, until he lost his seat in 1906 and retired from politics. He died in 1924.

Col. Robert Wright (after whom Wright's Hill is named) had bought land from Thomas Chamberlayne in 1854 at the eastern end of Weston Park, where he built Mayfield House two years later. He died in 1857 and the house remained the home of his widow and son Robert.

The 3rd Baron Radstock, an Irish peer whose family name was Waldegrave, purchased Mayfield House in 1889. He is best remembered for his evangelical work in Russia during the 1870s, a period when the Established Church there was at its lowest ebb. He preached at evening parties, usually in French, and his status as an English lord made him a fashionable 'high-class missionary'. Although his sermons were simple they proved popular among those who were only accustomed to the Orthodox Church and what had become a movement spread throughout the aristocracy. He left many converts, including tradesmen and artisans, as a testimony to his efforts.

A frugal man, he avoided all extravagance but would spend large sums of money on schemes to help the poor and took great care of his servants. He died of a heart attack on 8 December 1913. Radstock Road in Woolston perpetuates the family connection, as do the memorials in the south-

The Seaweed Hut, on the shore at the bottom of Weston Lane, c.1905. It was the Weston fishermen's net and gear store, with sides made of stout wood planks and the roof covered in seaweed. Now demolished, it is shown on early 17th-century nautical charts. Modern excavations confirmed that a concrete boat launching pad covers most of it, but the remaining base of the western planks was still accessible. The author had the pleasure of unearthing an 18th-century fisherman's clay pipe during these excavations. (Bill Moore)

Ladies from the Rolling Mills, c.1918. The 'Rolling Mills' on the Weston shoreline was established in the spring of 1916 by the Ministry of Munitions for the production of brass and cupro-nickel strip and this commenced in 1917. By 1918 there were 1,800 workers, of whom 650 were women. Most of them were local shop assistants or domestic servants, who, for the first time in their lives, received significant wages. The factory became the Royal Navy Stores Depot and in 1987, after the land had been sold for development, it was found that it was contaminated with asbestos and other dangerous waste. This was cleared, at considerable expense, prior to the construction of the present high-quality estate. (Bitterne Local History Society)

Mayfield House, with wounded soldiers being entertained by Lady Radstock, c.1915. It had 40 rooms, including 23 bedrooms, and was set in a 35-acre estate with 10 servants, including gardeners. Following the death of 78-year-old unmarried Granville, the 4th Baron, the estate was sold in 1937 to Southampton Corporation. It was opened as a public park on 23 June 1938, in accordance with a covenant in his will that it be kept as an open space. The beautiful mansion was used as temporary accommodation for the homeless during World War Two, but was so neglected that it was necessary to demolish it in 1956. (Bitterne Local History Society)

Erected in 1810 by William Chamberlayne in memory of the politician Charles James Fox, this obelisk was later dedicated by Robert Wright to two favourite horses, 'Workman' and 'Sally', who are buried nearby. Lord Radstock later inscribed the words 'The earth is the Lord's and the fullness thereof – Psalms 24.1' on it. Visible from his mansion, it was a constant reminder to him of the text. Before the current trees obscured it, it could be seen from what is now Obelisk Road and became the trademark of the local firm Lankester & Crook, whose headquarters were in that road.

Until 1855 the nearest place of worship for Weston residents was Jesus Chapel, Peartree, but in June that year a small building, known as 'Trinity Church', was built on the site of the present Solent Court by William Preston Hulton, one time incumbent of St Paul's Church in London Road, Southampton. He had inherited the Weston Park Barnfield estate on the death of his aunt. The present Holy Trinity Church replaced this building in 1865, on a site in Weston Lane given by Thomas Chamberlayne. It cost £4,700, met by William Preston Hulton, who died in 1870.

east corner of Holy Trinity Church, the wonderfully maintained flowerbeds in Mayfield's spacious grounds and the remaining stable block and clock tower.

Southampton had absorbed Weston as part of its eastern expansion in 1920 and plans were also made by the L&SW railway, which had acquired land on Weston Shore, to expand the docks into that area. Because of communication problems across the river the idea was shelved and the New Docks were constructed on the Millbrook side instead. Had the plan been realised, it would have resulted in a complete transformation of the area. However, a new road was planned in 1921 to run from Weston Grove to Netley, and this is now the shore road of Weston Shore with its fine sea view.

The first contract for Southampton's post-war permanent housing was for 100 houses at Weston Park and the first of these was built in Bramley Crescent in 1946. In the1960s large tower blocks of flats were built in International Way, overlooking Southampton Water and the New Forest, and were given the names of Copenhagen, Oslo, Le Havre and Rotterdam. This was a tribute to Councillor Reg Burns, who was not only in the forefront of the post-war housing development, but was the inspiring genius of the Southampton International Youth Rally, when young people from the Continent made exchange visits with the local youth.

Currently, more than two million pounds of government regeneration money is to be spent on the Weston Shore area. Plans include extensively refurbishing the tower blocks, to include an electronic concierge service in each tower. A new cycleway from Victoria Road in Woolston to Weston Parade is to be extended to make a continuous link to the Royal Victoria Country Park. New lighting and public toilets, traffic calming, upgraded play areas and the renovat-

The large tower blocks of International Way, Weston, with Mayfield Park and Sholing in the distance, *c.*1995. The residents have a fine view of the world's largest cruise liners and container ships across Southampton Water. *(Southern Daily Echo)*

ing of the shelters on the shore will all bring fresh life to the area. A new salt-water marsh is also to be created, along with other proposals to protect and encourage wildlife. Perhaps there will be a return to the pre-war days when the general public crowded the beach area during the summer months, emulating the south of France?

Further Reading

Fountain, David, *Lord Radstock of Mayfield*, Mayflower Christian Books, 1984.

Wise, Phillip, *A History of Holy Trinity*, 1990.

Woolston
including Itchen

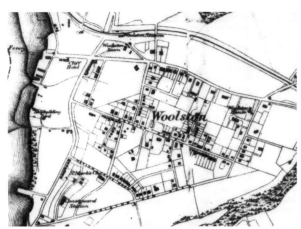

Woolston in 1870, showing the Cliff Hotel and Woolston Railway Station, built 1866. Note the coastguard station in the lower left corner, below St Mark's Church. Obelisk Road runs through the centre but the scattered detached houses are clearly of good quality. *(Reproduced from the 1870 Ordnance Survey map. NC/03/17894)*

THE general Itchen area, of which Woolston is a part, takes its name from the bordering River Itchen and has been associated with the Iceni tribe, recorded in a document of AD 701. Although its origin is uncertain it may well represent the name of a Celtic river god.

During the late 10th century the Vikings constantly attacked and pillaged the southern shores of England and in the harsh winter of 994 the armies of King Sweyn of Denmark and King Olaf of Norway were camped on the open lands of the Itchen area. It was here that the Bishop of Winchester persuaded Olaf to go to Andover to see King Ethelred the Unready, where he made his full acceptance of Christianity. It was during this confirmation that Olaf made a solemn vow never to return to England as an enemy, a vow that he kept. When he sailed away from his fortified 'tun' east of the river Itchen, he gave rise to the local belief that Woolston derives its name from 'Olafstun', thus accounting for the Viking badge on the

school blazers of Woolston Secondary School pupils. The Domesday Book of 1086 records Woolston as Olvestune, but the folio in which it would have been described is unfortunately blank. It is also possible, however, that the name comes from a 10th-century small farm in the area called Wulfic's Farm.

Little is known of the district during the ensuing years, until 1424 when a Richard Inkpenn conveyed the estate to his daughter Alice, wife of Ralph Chamberlayne, a surname that has been synonymous with the area since that time. However, in 1631 the estate was conveyed to Nathaniel Mills by Sir George Rivers and was said to consist of 'eight messuages, seven gardens, 150 acres of land, 50 acres of meady, 60 of pasture, 35 of woodland, 45 of furze and the passage over the River Itchen to Southampton'. This gives a good indication of the nature of the terrain at this time.

The right to ferry passengers across the Itchen between Southampton and Woolston was held by the fishermen of Itchen Ferry Village for many centuries. The Lords of the two Manors of Southampton and Woolston granted this privilege, the latter being paid in cash. The river passage granted to Nathaniel Mills was therefore a useful asset.

The development of Southampton as a spa at the end of the 18th century saw the area becoming attractive to the gentry, and William Chamberlayne, who owned most of the land in this region, created his adjacent Weston Grove Estate in 1802. This, with the opening up of new routes to Portsmouth via the new Northam Bridge; the commercial development and population increase in lower Southampton arising out of

The Cliff Hotel, Bridge Road, c.1895, when W. Gilchrist was the landlord. The building dates from the 1830s, when a coach service ran from outside. It was home to the original St Mary's Football Club (the Saints) in the 1890s. The author also enjoyed attending sessions of the Southampton Rhythm Club there in the 1950s. It closed prior to 1990. *(Bitterne Local History Society)*

No longer a hotel in 2004 but an apartment block with a nice view of the adjacent River Itchen.

The Itchen Bridge in 2003, taken from the Woolston side of the river. The massive span beams were actually cast on top of the bridge and transferred to a launching system made up of girder sections and hydraulic bogies. The launching girders were pulled across the gap between the support piers onto a nosing on the far side. The whole concrete span was then pulled across on the hydraulic bogies until it was in the exact position and then lowered onto jacks. Each cantilever arm had to remain carefully and precisely balanced, but as one can see, the tricky operations proceeded smoothly. The 61,000-ton bridge was opened for the first time to pedestrians on Tuesday 31 May 1977 and officially opened by HRH Princess Alexandra on the ensuing 13 July.

the proposed docks construction; and the consequent increased value of the land on the eastern bank, all resulted in strong pressures for a new and better crossing in the lower Itchen area.

The Itchen Bridge Company was thus formed in 1833, with the express purpose of building a bridge to rival that at Northam, but with lower tolls. It was to join Crosshouse with Itchen Village, on the line of the ancient Itchen ferry. The first design was that of a bridge having 17 spans, one of which could swing to allow shipping to pass. However, the Admiralty decided that this would hinder navigation and the plans were dropped.

The Company were not to be defeated and contacted James Meadows Rendel, a Plymouth engineer who had built wooden steam-powered floating bridges, hauled across on chains, at Dartmouth and Saltash. The Itchen gentry showed great interest in this scheme and contributed nearly a third of the capital on the first subscription list in 1834. Thomas Chamberlayne, part owner of the Crosshouse ferry and owner of most of Woolston and Weston, gave his interest in the

The Floating Bridges in 1908, taken on the town side of the River Itchen and looking towards Woolston. The spire of St Mary's Presbyterian Church in Portsmouth Road can be seen in the background. It was demolished in 1972 and a supermarket now stands on the site.

Portsmouth Road, Woolston, c.1895, showing the advert of D. Chill, Pawnbroker, and the corner offices of William Henry Bell, Solicitor and Clerk to the old Itchen Urban District Council. On the left, on the corner of Victoria Road, is the London Arms, built in the early 1870s. It was destroyed in 1940 and rebuilt after the war but is currently scheduled for redevelopment. *(Norman Gardiner Collection – Bitterne Local History Society)*

common lands over which the proposed new road to Bursledon would pass, as well as materials from his commons for the repair of the roads for the ensuing 20 years.

After some initial problems, due to competition from the upstream Northam Bridge Company, the floating bridges became an essential trading route and replaced the rowing boats of the Itchen Ferrymen, who had mainly catered for local traffic. Two foot-passenger bridges were built in 1879 and 1881 but by 1902 these had been replaced by three more combined foot-passenger and carriage bridges. By now the hours of service had been extended from 5.30am to 12.30am. Two bridges ran simultaneously, crossing in midstream and providing a seven and a half minute service. The main road leading east to Portsmouth, from the landing hard of the floating bridges, continued to be, and remains, the heart of Woolston.

Artisans' houses were built along Bridge Road and Mortimer Road during this period, together with similar housing in Victoria, St Johns, Inkerman and Florence Roads, catering for the industrial shipbuilding that had developed on the southern shore of Woolston. Millais Road in Itchen later commemorated one of Southampton's famous sons. Born in Southampton's Portland Street in 1829, Sir John Everett Millais was an artist of the Pre-Raphaelite School and is buried in St Paul's Cathedral.

Churches also appeared to serve the increasing population; St Mark's in 1863, the Obelisk Road Wesleyan in 1864, followed by St Mary's Presbyterian in 1876 and the Roman Catholic St Patrick's Church in 1884.

The railway line to Netley, via Woolston and Sholing, gave rise to the building of Woolston Station in 1866, further improving the area's communications. This increasing development

Celebrating the 11 November Armistice Day, 1918, in lower Portsmouth Road at the junction with Bridge Road. The Revd and Mrs Ashdown are looking over the Vicarage wall, now replaced by a parade of shops. Opposite can be seen, left to right, White's Fruit Stores; the Corn Exchange (home to Gamble & Chalk, Corn & Coal Merchants); Mr Grimshaw's Dental Surgery and a chemist. *(Joan Holt)*

Shop assistants proudly stand outside their Co-operative Society store at 35/37 Victoria Road, *c.*1925. Unlike the other multiple business changes in the city, this store remains unchanged, except now it is a Co-op Self-Service Supermarket. *(Bitterne Local History Society)*

led to an attempt by the borough to annexe Woolston in 1895, when it took in Bitterne Park, Banister, Freemantle and Shirley. However, this failed after a public enquiry supported the residents' resistance to a change in their rural status.

The Floating Bridge Company's fortunes continued to prosper throughout World War One and after the Borough of Southampton succeeded in absorbing Itchen in 1920 there was political pressure to free all the river crossings from toll. When Northam Bridge was acquired by the Corporation and freed from toll in 1929 this naturally seriously affected the traffic on the floating bridges. After long negotiations the Floating

Nos 214 to 220 Manor Road after a parachute mine fell nearby in November 1940, killing 15 residents. These are a typical example of the 12,516 homes that were damaged or destroyed in Southampton during the *blitzkrieg* of World War Two. *(Southampton Archive Services)*

One o'clock at Thornycrofts, *c.*1920. Shipyard workers disgorging from the works were a familiar and comforting sight to the local shopkeepers. In January 1928 the joiners' shop and moulding loft were destroyed in a major fire, with the fierce heat damaging some of the houses opposite. The terraced houses have hardly changed, but the shipyard complex is about to undergo dramatic transformation now the company has left the district. (*Bitterne Local History Society*)

Bridge Company eventually sold out in 1934 and the bridges entered into Corporation ownership.

A red-letter day came in September 1946 when the bridges were made free from toll for foot passengers, cyclists and prams! However, wear and tear on the bridges increasingly led to breakdowns and in 1961 the Corporation was compelled to obtain a new replacement diesel-powered bridge, followed by two more as the anticipated building of a high-level bridge was constantly deferred. There had always been demands for a fixed bridge across the river at Woolston and a year after the opening of the new dual carriageway Northam Bridge in 1954, attention was once again directed towards such a bridge.

Matters were delayed for various reasons but a 1960 Act provided powers for the compulsory purchase of properties, to both create appropriate approach roads on both sides of the river and to provide areas for the actual construction pro-

cesses. This blighted the land on both sides of the river, restricting development and planning and leaving many properties derelict and the areas in a state of limbo. Important factors in the minds of the Council were that a very expensive refit or replacement of the three floating bridges would be required by the late 1970s, and their compulsory purchase powers would expire in 1973.

This concentrated the minds of Councillors on the need for positive action and on 2 July 1970 the decision was taken to proceed with the bridge on the basis that it would now have to produce revenue from a toll. Thus, at long last, the die was cast and what up to now had only been recommendations were transformed into action. The original Consultant Engineers, R. Travers Morgan, prepared plans, feasibility studies and costs of seven alternative bridge layouts. The scheme eventually chosen was just upstream of the floating bridges and involved five spans, two

Vosper Thornycroft, from the Itchen Bridge in 2003. In June, 2003, HMS *Mersey*, an off-shore patrol vessel, slipped into the water as the last Royal Navy ship to be built at Southampton, signalling the end of an era.

of 262ft and three of 410ft. Suspended spans would rest on cantilevers 151ft out from each pier. Kier Limited's lowest tender of £5,710,630 was quickly accepted.

A good deal of advance work had to be carried out, with land either side purchased and cleared. The resultant demolitions presented a sorry sight for many months but on the morning of 22 March 1974 the Mayor, Alderman Michael Pettet, ceremoniously drove in the first pile for the bridge's foundations on the Woolston side of the river and work then commenced.

Dramatic changes were simultaneously taking place on both sides of the river. The junction between Oakbank Road and Bridge Road was realigned; a new roundabout was constructed at the Portsmouth Road junction with Manor Road, and the new bridge approach road was prepared to accommodate the toll plaza with its five-toll lane. A pedestrian subway under the bridge

approach embankment also created a link between Woolston Railway Station, Portsmouth Road and Bridge Road. On the Chapel side a new roundabout was created at the junction of Lower Bridge Road.

The sad end to the familiar floating bridges came in June 1977 when the Itchen Bridge finally came into use and the last floating bridge crossing, accompanied by crowds of well wishers, took place.

However, the main local industry and focal point of the area has been shipbuilding along the shoreline. This had been widespread on the west bank of the Itchen since the 17th century, but a boom in demand for large iron sailing ships in the 1870s saw the first Woolston yard established by Thomas Ridley Oswald in 1876. His first iron vessel in the yard was the 853-ton 191ft-long barque *Aberfoyle*. The firm changed to Oswald, Mordaunt & Co. when he took a partner in 1878 and turned out over 104 sailing cargo ships before it closed in 1889.

Shipbuilding at Woolston remained spasmodic, until John I. Thornycroft left his shipyard at Chiswick in 1904 and moved to Woolston. This was the beginning of one of the great names in British maritime history, the more so when it merged with the Portsmouth firm of Vosper in the mid-1960s. It continues to hold the highest international reputation for building naval vessels that are in the vanguard of cutting-edge design and its ships are renowned throughout the world.

The Woolston Millennium Garden, opened April 2002, has a central theme of flight and float, with a 10-metre high feather sculpture of stainless steel and recycled glass as a focal point. The garden around it is divided into three by a propeller-shaped brick path, each brick inscribed with a name and/or date of local significance. The three segments represent land, sea and sky and the steel backing walls are in the shape of a Supermarine Spitfire's wing and a Vosper Thornycroft trimaran 'Triton'.

In the heart of Woolston, Thornycrofts provided continued employment for generations of local workers and the echoing noise of riveting was a familiar sound to residents during the building of over 600 ships in the Woolston yard. Among these was the famous HMS *Kelly*, commanded by Lord Louis Mountbatten during World War Two.

Sadly, Woolston proved to be too small for the construction of the Navy's latest class of warship and in early 2004 the company relocated to a purpose-built complex at Portsmouth Naval Base. The 33-acre site was sold for £15 million and plans are currently being considered for a mixture of commercial and residential development on this attractive waterfront position, ideally located for Woolston's resident population of around 16,000.

It remains to be seen how this exciting project is finally resolved to replace the loss of the famous Vosper Thornycroft yard that had become a way of life for many generations.

Further Reading

Adams, Brian *The Missing Link,* Southampton City Council, 1977.

Brown, Jim *Bridging the Itchen,* Bitterne Local History Society, 2002.

Cleverley, Audrey *Focus On Woolston,* Sholing Press, 1980.

Ford, Ken *A Funny Thing Happened on the Way to the Launch,* Privately printed, 1987.

Hartley, G.A. *The Parish of St Patrick, Southampton, 1879–1984,* F. Wilson, 1985.

Local Studies Group, *Woolston & Sholing,* 1984.

Mornington, Gerald *Southampton's Marquis and other Mariners,* Dorset Publishing Co., 1984.

O'Dell, Noreen *The River Itchen,* Paul Cave Publications, 1977.

Oral History Team *Woolston Before The Bridge,* Southampton City Council, 1989.

Rance Adrian *Shipbuilding in Victorian Southampton,* Southampton University Industrial Archaeology Group, 1981.

Slade, Eileen *Yesterday Becomes Tomorrow,* Southampton University, 1982.

St Mark's Woolston Millennium Group *Woolston Parish,* St Mark's Vicarage, 1999.

Index

Changes to street names

The following name changes are known to have taken place at different periods of Southampton's history, consequent upon various suburbs being brought into the then County Borough of Southampton. Problems were quickly encountered with identical road names and within a year or so changes were implemented.

Current name	Original name	Date
Almatade Road	Alma Road, Bitterne	1924
Almond Road	Alma Road, Shirley	1902
Anglesea Road	Brunswick Road, Shirley	c.1900
Augustine Road	Oak Road, NorthamI	1924
Beatrice Road	Victoria Road, Shirley	1924
Bellemoor Road	Upper Shirley Road	1883
Bernard Street	Bridge Street	1924
Bishops Road	High Street, Itchen	1924
Bitterne Road East (part)	Botley Road, Bitterne	
Bourne Road	Osbourne Road, Freemantle	1898
Burgess Road (previously Street)	Alma Road, Bassett	1924
Bursledon Road (part)	Church Road, Bitterne	
Cannon Street	Pound Street, Shirley	1924
Carlisle Road	Union Road, Shirley	1903
Cawte Road	Union Road, Freemantle	1903
Chatsworth Road	Victoria Road, Bitterne	1924
Church Lane	Portswood Back Lane	
Cracknore Road	Lodge Road, Freemantle	1901
Deacon Road	Furze Lane, Bitterne	
Deacon Road (part)	Thornhill Road, Bitterne	1924
Dean Road (part)	Brewery Road, Bitterne	
Dean Road (part)	Chapel Street, Bitterne	1924
Florence Road	Alma Road, Woolston	1924
Glen Road	Grove Road, Woolston	1924
Hawkeswood Road	South View Road, Bitterne	post-1918
Hazel Road	Elm Road, Itchen	1924
Hewitts Road	Cliff Road, Freemantle	c.1900
Howards Grove	Pound Road, Shirley	c.1900
Kathleen Road	St Mary Street, Sholing	1924
Kentish Road	Kent Road, Shirley	1903
Keswick Road	Albert Road, Woolston	1924
Laurel Road	Ivy Road, Itchen	1924
Manor Farm Road	Holland Road, Bitterne	
Marlborough Road	Oxford Street, Shirley	1924

Marne Road	Inkerman Road, Bitterne	1924
Midanbury Lane (part)	Dott's Lane, Bitterne	post-1911
Oakley Road	Mousehole Lane, Shirley	*c.*1900
Ozier Road	Love Lane, Bitterne	1966
Parkville Road	Park Road, Swaythling	1924
Paynes/Park Roads (part)	Naseby Road, Freemantle	1904
Pinegrove Road	Firgrove Road, Sholing	1924
Pitt Road	Lake Road, Freemantle	1924
Poole Road	Brook Road, Itchen	1924
Pound Street	Pound Lane, Bitterne	1897
Radstock Road	Avenue Road, Itchen	1924
Randolph Street	Russell Street, Shirley	1903
Redcar Street	Regent Street, Shirley	1903
Roberts Road	Albert Road, Shirley	1901
Ruby Road	Lodge Road, Bitterne	1924
Rupert Road	Albert Road, Bitterne	1924
Sandringham Road	The Crescent, Bitterne Park	1924
Sea Road	Hill Street, Itchen	1924
Shales Road	Back Lane, Bitterne	
Shirley Road	Romsey Lane, Freemantle	*c.*1900
Spring Crescent	Spring Road, Portswood	1924
Spring Road	Merryoak Lane	
St Anne's Road	Milton Road, Woolston	1924
St Edmund's Road	Leighton Road, Shirley	1924
	(Changed from Oxford Road *c.*1900)	
St Monica Road	Church Road, Sholing	1924
Stratton Road	(Police) Station Road, Shirley	1903
Swift Road	Onslow Road, Woolston	1924
Tankerville Road	Britannia Road, Itchen	1924
Thornhill Road	Back Lane (known locally)	by 1987
University Road	Back Lane, Highfield	
Vaudrey Street	Beavis Street, Shirley	1901
Vespasian Road	Clausentum Road, Bitterne	1924
Victor Street	Albert Street, Shirley	1901
Walpole Road	Avenue Road, Itchen	1924
Warren Crescent	The Crescent, Shirley Warren	1924
Wharncliffe Road	Cliff Road, Woolston	1924
Wolseley Road	Wellington Road, Shirley	1903

ND - #0369 - 270225 - C0 - 260/195/10 - PB - 9781780913261 - Gloss Lamination